WHY WE LOVE

The Nature, Source, and Chemistry of Romantic Love

Dr. Maxwell Shimba

Printed in the United States of America

SHIMBA
PUBLISHING

TABLE OF CONTENTS

INTRODUCTION

The Essence of Romantic Love

Romantic love is a universal human experience, deeply embedded in the fabric of our lives and culture. It transcends boundaries of race, nationality, and religion, touching the hearts and minds of people around the world. Despite its ubiquitous presence, romantic love remains one of the most complex and enigmatic aspects of human existence. It is a powerful force that can inspire profound joy, drive personal growth, and even heal wounds, yet it can also lead to heartache, conflict, and despair.

The journey to understand romantic love takes us through a rich tapestry of scientific discovery, psychological insight, cultural expression, and spiritual reflection. In this book, we will explore the nature and chemistry of romantic love, uncovering the biological mechanisms that drive it, the psychological dimensions that shape it, and the spiritual elements that elevate it.

Defining Romantic Love

Romantic love is often characterized by intense emotions, strong physical attraction, and a deep sense of connection with another person. It involves a unique blend of passion, intimacy, and commitment that distinguishes it from other forms of love, such as familial or platonic love.

Romantic love can spark instantaneously or develop gradually over time, and it often involves a desire for exclusivity and long-term partnership.

While the experience of romantic love is highly personal and subjective, there are common elements that many people share. These include a longing to be close to the beloved, a sense of joy and fulfillment when together, and a willingness to sacrifice for the relationship's well-being. Romantic love can be both exhilarating and challenging, as it requires vulnerability, trust, and continuous effort to maintain.

The Significance of Romantic Love in Human Life

Romantic love plays a crucial role in human life, influencing our behavior, decisions, and overall well-being. It is a driving force behind the formation of families and the continuation of our species. Beyond its biological imperative, romantic love enriches our lives in countless ways. It provides emotional support, companionship, and a sense of belonging. It motivates us to become better versions of ourselves, fostering personal growth and self-discovery.

In many ways, romantic love is a mirror that reflects our deepest desires, fears, and aspirations. It challenges us to confront our insecurities, embrace our strengths, and navigate the complexities of human relationships. The experience of loving and being loved can bring profound meaning and purpose to our lives, enhancing our emotional and psychological resilience.

Themes of Nature, Chemistry, and Spiritual Dimensions of Love

To truly understand romantic love, we must delve into its multifaceted nature. This book is structured around three central themes: the nature of love, the chemistry of love, and the spiritual dimensions of love.

1. The Nature of Love: This theme explores the evolutionary and psychological foundations of romantic love. We will examine why humans have evolved to experience love, how love influences our behavior and relationships, and the different stages and types of romantic love. By understanding the natural basis of love, we can gain insights into its universal characteristics and individual variations.

2. The Chemistry of Love: Romantic love is not just an abstract feeling; it is deeply rooted in our biology. This theme investigates the neurochemical and hormonal processes that underpin romantic attraction, attachment, and bonding. We will explore how brain chemistry drives the feelings of euphoria, desire, and connection that define romantic love, and how these processes can affect our thoughts and actions.

3. The Spiritual Dimensions of Love: Beyond its physical and psychological aspects, romantic love has a profound spiritual dimension. This theme delves into the ways that love intersects with spirituality, faith, and personal growth. We will explore how different cultures and religions view romantic love, the role of love in spiritual practices, and the ways in which love can lead to a deeper understanding of ourselves and the world around us.

Conclusion

Romantic love is a complex and multifaceted phenomenon that touches every aspect of our lives. By exploring its nature, chemistry, and spiritual dimensions, we can gain a deeper understanding of why we love and how love shapes our existence. This book invites you on a journey to uncover the mysteries of romantic love, offering insights and reflections that can enhance your appreciation of this powerful and transformative force.

As we embark on this exploration, let us keep in mind that love, in all its forms, is a fundamental aspect of the human experience. It is a source of joy and fulfillment, a catalyst for personal growth, and a beacon of hope in our lives. By understanding the nature and chemistry of romantic love, we can better navigate the challenges and opportunities it presents, enriching our relationships and our lives.

DR. MAXWELL SHIMBA

CHAPTER 01

EVOLUTIONARY PERSPECTIVE OF ROMANTIC LOVE

Romantic love, with its profound emotions and intense connections, is a deeply rooted aspect of human existence. But why did humans evolve to experience such powerful feelings? To understand this, we need to delve into evolutionary theories that explain the adaptive functions of romantic love and its role in human survival and reproduction. By exploring these theories, we can uncover the biological imperatives that have shaped the way we love and bond with one another.

The Evolutionary Basis of Romantic Love

Evolutionary biology provides a framework for understanding the origins and functions of romantic love. At its core, romantic love can be seen as an adaptive strategy that has evolved to enhance reproductive success and ensure the survival of offspring. This strategy involves a combination of mate selection, pair bonding, and cooperative parenting, all of which are crucial for the continuation of our species.

Mate Selection

One of the primary functions of romantic love is to facilitate mate selection. From an evolutionary perspective, choosing the right partner is critical for reproductive success. Romantic love plays a key role in this process by creating a strong attraction to potential mates who possess desirable traits, such as physical health, fertility, and genetic compatibility.

Charles Darwin's theory of sexual selection highlights the importance of mate choice in evolution. According to this theory, individuals with traits that are attractive to potential mates are more likely to reproduce and pass on their genes. Romantic love, with its emphasis on attraction and desire, can be seen as a mechanism that drives sexual selection, helping individuals find and secure high-quality mates.

Pair Bonding

Beyond mate selection, romantic love also fosters pair bonding, a long-term attachment between partners that is essential for raising offspring. In many species, including humans, cooperative parenting significantly increases the chances of offspring survival. Romantic love strengthens the emotional and physical bonds between partners, promoting cooperation and stability within the relationship.

The evolutionary significance of pair bonding is evident in the behavior of monogamous species. For example, many birds and mammals form long-term bonds with a single mate, working together to protect and nurture their young. In humans, romantic love supports pair bonding by creating a deep sense of connection, trust, and mutual dependence, which are vital for successful parenting.

Cooperative Parenting

Romantic love not only facilitates mate selection and pair bonding but also promotes cooperative parenting. Raising human children requires a considerable investment of time, energy, and resources. Romantic love encourages parents to work together in providing care, protection, and guidance to their offspring.

This cooperative effort is crucial for the development and well-being of children, who are highly dependent on their caregivers for an extended period. By fostering strong emotional bonds between parents, romantic love ensures that both partners remain committed to the parenting role, increasing the likelihood of their children's survival and eventual reproductive success.

The Neurobiological Mechanisms of Romantic Love

To understand the evolutionary basis of romantic love, it is essential to explore the neurobiological mechanisms that underpin it. Romantic love is associated with specific brain regions and neurochemical processes that drive attraction, attachment, and bonding.

Dopamine and Reward

Dopamine, a neurotransmitter associated with the brain's reward system, plays a central role in romantic love. When we experience romantic attraction, dopamine levels increase, creating feelings of pleasure, excitement, and euphoria. This neurochemical response reinforces behaviors that lead to romantic and sexual encounters, promoting mate selection and bonding.

Research using brain imaging techniques has shown that areas of the brain rich in dopamine receptors, such as the ventral tegmental area (VTA) and the caudate nucleus, are highly active when individuals view images of their romantic partners. This suggests that romantic love activates the brain's reward circuitry, motivating individuals to seek and maintain romantic relationships.

Oxytocin and Attachment

Oxytocin, often referred to as the "love hormone," is another critical player in the neurobiology of romantic love. This hormone is released during physical touch, sexual activity, and childbirth, promoting feelings of closeness and bonding between partners. Oxytocin enhances trust and empathy, key components of stable and cooperative relationships.

Studies have shown that higher levels of oxytocin are associated with increased relationship satisfaction and stability. For example, couples who exhibit higher levels of oxytocin during interactions tend to report stronger emotional bonds and greater relationship longevity. This hormone's role in facilitating attachment and bonding highlights its evolutionary importance in romantic love.

Vasopressin and Monogamy

Vasopressin, another hormone related to social behavior, also plays a role in romantic love and monogamy. Research on prairie voles, a monogamous species, has shown that vasopressin receptors in the brain are linked to pair bonding and mate guarding behaviors. In humans, variations in vasopressin receptor genes have been associated with differences in relationship behaviors and attachment styles.

The presence of vasopressin and its influence on monogamy suggest that this hormone contributes to the stability and exclusivity of romantic relationships. By promoting behaviors that support long-term bonding and cooperative parenting, vasopressin enhances the evolutionary benefits of romantic love.

The Role of Culture in Shaping Romantic Love

While the biological and evolutionary underpinnings of romantic love are significant, it is essential to recognize the role of culture in shaping how we experience and express love. Cultural norms, values, and traditions influence our perceptions of romantic love, affecting everything from mate selection to relationship dynamics.

Cultural Variations in Mate Selection

Different cultures have diverse criteria for mate selection, reflecting societal values and priorities. For example, in some cultures, arranged marriages are common, with families playing a central role in choosing partners based on social status, economic stability, and compatibility. In contrast, other cultures emphasize individual choice and romantic attraction as the primary factors in mate selection.

These cultural variations highlight the interplay between biological drives and social influences in shaping romantic love. While the underlying neurobiological mechanisms of love are universal, the ways in which we pursue and maintain romantic relationships are profoundly affected by cultural context.

Cultural Norms and Relationship Dynamics

Cultural norms also dictate the acceptable behaviors and expectations within romantic relationships. These norms can influence everything from courtship practices and expressions of affection to gender roles and power dynamics. Understanding the cultural context of romantic love allows us to appreciate the diversity of human relationships and the ways in which love is experienced across different societies.

For instance, some cultures place a strong emphasis on collectivism and family cohesion, prioritizing the needs of the group over individual desires. In such cultures, romantic relationships are often viewed within the context of broader family and community networks. Conversely, cultures that value individualism may prioritize personal fulfillment and self-expression within romantic relationships.

Conclusion

Romantic love is a multifaceted phenomenon with deep evolutionary roots. By facilitating mate selection, pair bonding, and cooperative parenting, romantic love has played a crucial role in human survival and reproductive success. The neurobiological mechanisms underlying love, including the roles of dopamine, oxytocin, and vasopressin, highlight the intricate interplay between biology and behavior in shaping our romantic experiences.

While evolutionary theories provide a foundational understanding of why we love, it is essential to consider the cultural influences that shape our perceptions and expressions of romantic love. By exploring both the biological imperatives and cultural contexts of love, we can gain a comprehensive understanding of this powerful and transformative force in human life.

As we continue our journey through this book, we will delve deeper into the psychological dimensions, chemistry, and spiritual aspects of romantic love, uncovering the many layers that contribute to our experience of love and connection.

Evolutionary Perspectives on Romantic Love

Romantic love, with its profound emotions and intense connections, is a deeply rooted aspect of human existence. But why did humans evolve to experience such powerful feelings? To understand this, we need to delve into evolutionary theories that explain the adaptive functions of romantic love and its role in human survival and reproduction. By exploring these theories, we can uncover the biological imperatives that have shaped the way we love and bond with one another.

The Evolutionary Basis of Romantic Love

Evolutionary biology provides a framework for understanding the origins and functions of romantic love. At its core, romantic love can be seen as an adaptive strategy that has evolved to enhance reproductive success and ensure the survival of offspring. This strategy involves a combination of mate selection, pair bonding, and cooperative parenting, all of which are crucial for the continuation of our species.

Mate Selection

One of the primary functions of romantic love is to facilitate mate selection. From an evolutionary perspective, choosing the right partner is critical for reproductive success. Romantic love plays a key role in this process by creating a strong attraction to potential mates who possess desirable traits, such as physical health, fertility, and genetic compatibility.

Charles Darwin's theory of sexual selection highlights the importance of mate choice in evolution. According to this theory, individuals with traits that are attractive to potential mates are more likely to reproduce and pass on their genes. Romantic love, with its emphasis on attraction and desire, can be seen as a mechanism that drives sexual selection, helping individuals find and secure high-quality mates.

Pair Bonding

Beyond mate selection, romantic love also fosters pair bonding, a long-term attachment between partners that is essential for raising offspring. In many species, including humans, cooperative parenting significantly increases the chances of offspring survival. Romantic love strengthens the emotional and physical bonds between partners, promoting cooperation and stability within the relationship.

The evolutionary significance of pair bonding is evident in the behavior of monogamous species. For example, many birds and mammals form long-term bonds with a single mate, working together to protect and nurture their young. In humans, romantic love supports pair bonding by creating a deep sense of connection, trust, and mutual dependence, which are vital for successful parenting.

Cooperative Parenting

Romantic love not only facilitates mate selection and pair bonding but also promotes cooperative parenting. Raising human children requires a considerable investment of time, energy, and resources. Romantic love encourages parents to work together in providing care, protection, and guidance to their offspring.

This cooperative effort is crucial for the development and well-being of children, who are highly dependent on their caregivers for an extended period. By fostering strong emotional bonds between parents, romantic love ensures that both partners remain committed to the parenting role, increasing the likelihood of their children's survival and eventual reproductive success.

The Neurobiological Mechanisms of Romantic Love

To understand the evolutionary basis of romantic love, it is essential to explore the neurobiological mechanisms that underpin it. Romantic love is associated with specific brain regions and neurochemical processes that drive attraction, attachment, and bonding.

Dopamine and Reward

Dopamine, a neurotransmitter associated with the brain's reward system, plays a central role in romantic love. When we experience romantic attraction, dopamine levels increase, creating feelings of pleasure, excitement, and euphoria. This neurochemical response reinforces behaviors that lead to romantic and sexual encounters, promoting mate selection and bonding.

Research using brain imaging techniques has shown that areas of the brain rich in dopamine receptors, such as the ventral tegmental area (VTA) and the caudate nucleus, are highly active when individuals view images of their romantic partners. This suggests that romantic love activates the brain's reward circuitry, motivating individuals to seek and maintain romantic relationships.

Oxytocin and Attachment

Oxytocin, often referred to as the "love hormone," is another critical player in the neurobiology of romantic love. This hormone is released during physical touch, sexual activity, and childbirth, promoting feelings of closeness and bonding between partners. Oxytocin enhances trust and empathy, key components of stable and cooperative relationships.

Studies have shown that higher levels of oxytocin are associated with increased relationship satisfaction and stability. For example, couples who exhibit higher levels of oxytocin during interactions tend to report stronger emotional bonds and greater relationship longevity. This hormone's role in facilitating attachment and bonding highlights its evolutionary importance in romantic love.

Vasopressin and Monogamy

Vasopressin, another hormone related to social behavior, also plays a role in romantic love and monogamy. Research on prairie voles, a monogamous species, has shown that vasopressin receptors in the brain are linked to pair bonding and mate guarding behaviors. In humans, variations in vasopressin receptor genes have been associated with differences in relationship behaviors and attachment styles.

The presence of vasopressin and its influence on monogamy suggest that this hormone contributes to the stability and exclusivity of romantic relationships. By promoting behaviors that support long-term bonding and cooperative parenting, vasopressin enhances the evolutionary benefits of romantic love.

The Role of Culture in Shaping Romantic Love

While the biological and evolutionary underpinnings of romantic love are significant, it is essential to recognize the role of culture in shaping how we experience and express love. Cultural norms, values, and traditions influence our perceptions of romantic love, affecting everything from mate selection to relationship dynamics.

Cultural Variations in Mate Selection

Different cultures have diverse criteria for mate selection, reflecting societal values and priorities. For example, in some cultures, arranged marriages are common, with families playing a central role in choosing partners based on social status, economic stability, and compatibility. In contrast, other cultures emphasize individual choice and romantic attraction as the primary factors in mate selection.

These cultural variations highlight the interplay between biological drives and social influences in shaping romantic love. While the underlying neurobiological mechanisms of love are universal, the ways in which we pursue and maintain romantic relationships are profoundly affected by cultural context.

Cultural Norms and Relationship Dynamics

Cultural norms also dictate the acceptable behaviors and expectations within romantic relationships. These norms can influence everything from courtship practices and expressions of affection to gender roles and power dynamics. Understanding the cultural context of romantic love allows us to appreciate the diversity of human relationships and the ways in which love is experienced across different societies.

For instance, some cultures place a strong emphasis on collectivism and family cohesion, prioritizing the needs of the group over individual desires. In such cultures, romantic relationships are often viewed within the context of broader family and community networks. Conversely, cultures that value individualism may prioritize personal fulfillment and self-expression within romantic relationships.

Conclusion

Romantic love is a multifaceted phenomenon with deep evolutionary roots. By facilitating mate selection, pair bonding, and cooperative parenting, romantic love has played a crucial role in human survival and reproductive success. The neurobiological mechanisms underlying love, including the roles of dopamine, oxytocin, and vasopressin, highlight the intricate interplay between biology and behavior in shaping our romantic experiences.

While evolutionary theories provide a foundational understanding of why we love, it is essential to consider the cultural influences that shape our perceptions and expressions of romantic love. By exploring both the biological imperatives and cultural contexts of love, we can gain a comprehensive understanding of this powerful and transformative force in human life.

As we continue our journey through this book, we will delve deeper into the psychological dimensions, chemistry, and spiritual aspects of romantic love, uncovering the many layers that contribute to our experience of love and connection.

CHAPTER 02

PSYCHOLOGICAL DIMENSIONS OF ROMANTIC LOVE

While evolutionary biology provides insights into the origins and adaptive functions of romantic love, psychology offers a detailed understanding of how love operates within the human mind. Psychological theories explore the components of romantic love—attachment, intimacy, and commitment—and how these elements interact to shape our relationships. By examining these dimensions, we can gain a deeper understanding of the complexities and dynamics of romantic love.

Attachment: The Foundation of Romantic Bonds

Attachment theory, developed by John Bowlby and later expanded by Mary Ainsworth, provides a framework for understanding the emotional bonds that form between romantic partners. Originally formulated to explain the bond between infants and their caregivers, attachment theory has been adapted to explore adult romantic relationships.

Types of Attachment

Attachment styles, formed during early childhood, significantly influence how individuals approach romantic relationships. There are four primary attachment styles:

1. Secure Attachment: Individuals with secure attachment styles tend to have healthy, trusting relationships. They are comfortable with intimacy and independence, and they exhibit confidence in their partner's love and support.

2. Anxious-Preoccupied Attachment: Those with an anxious-preoccupied attachment style often seek high levels of intimacy, approval, and responsiveness from their partners. They may be overly dependent on their partner and experience intense fear of abandonment.

3. Dismissive-Avoidant Attachment: Individuals with a dismissive-avoidant attachment style prioritize independence and self-reliance. They may avoid emotional closeness and have difficulty depending on others, often leading to emotional distance in relationships.

4. Fearful-Avoidant Attachment: This attachment style, also known as disorganized attachment, is characterized by a combination of fear and desire for intimacy. Individuals

may have a history of trauma or inconsistent caregiving, leading to unpredictable and often turbulent relationships.

Influence on Romantic Relationships

Attachment styles profoundly affect how individuals perceive and behave in romantic relationships. Securely attached individuals are more likely to experience stable and fulfilling relationships, characterized by mutual trust, effective communication, and emotional support. In contrast, those with insecure attachment styles (anxious, avoidant, or fearful) may struggle with relationship stability and satisfaction, often experiencing cycles of conflict and distress.

Intimacy: The Emotional Connection

Intimacy is a core component of romantic love, encompassing the emotional closeness and deep connection that partners share. Psychologist Robert Sternberg, in his Triangular Theory of Love, identifies intimacy as one of the three primary components of love, alongside passion and commitment.

Building Intimacy

Intimacy involves several key elements:

1. Emotional Sharing: Partners in intimate relationships openly share their thoughts, feelings, and experiences. This emotional transparency fosters a sense of understanding and closeness.

2. Vulnerability: Intimacy requires a willingness to be vulnerable with one another. By revealing their true selves, including fears and insecurities, partners build trust and deepen their connection.

3. Mutual Respect: Respecting each other's individuality and boundaries is essential for maintaining intimacy. This respect allows partners to feel valued and supported.

4. Quality Time: Spending meaningful time together strengthens the emotional bond between partners. Engaging in shared activities and creating memories enhances intimacy.

Challenges to Intimacy

Despite its importance, maintaining intimacy can be challenging. Life stressors, communication barriers, and unresolved conflicts can erode emotional closeness. Additionally, individuals with insecure attachment styles may find it difficult to establish and sustain intimate connections. Addressing these challenges through effective communication, empathy, and mutual effort is crucial for preserving intimacy in romantic relationships.

Commitment: The Decision to Love

Commitment represents the decision to maintain and nurture a romantic relationship over time. It involves a conscious choice to invest in the partnership, work through difficulties, and plan for a shared future. Sternberg's Triangular Theory of Love highlights commitment as a crucial component of enduring love.

Factors Influencing Commitment

Several factors contribute to the level of commitment in a relationship:

1. Satisfaction: Relationship satisfaction, including emotional fulfillment, sexual satisfaction, and compatibility, influences commitment. Partners who are satisfied with their relationship are more likely to remain committed.

2. Investment: The time, energy, and resources invested in the relationship play a significant role in commitment. The more partners invest, the more likely they are to stay committed.

3. Alternatives: Perceptions of available alternatives impact commitment. If individuals believe they have better romantic options outside their current relationship, their commitment may wane.

4. Social and Cultural Influences: Societal norms, cultural values, and social support systems can reinforce or challenge commitment. For example, cultures that emphasize the importance of marriage and family may foster stronger commitment in relationships.

Commitment and Relationship Stability

Commitment is a key predictor of relationship stability and longevity. High levels of commitment encourage partners to work through conflicts, support each other through challenges, and prioritize the relationship's well-being. Conversely, low commitment can lead to relationship instability, increased conflict, and a higher likelihood of dissolution.

The Interaction of Attachment, Intimacy, and Commitment

The components of romantic love—attachment, intimacy, and commitment—are interrelated and collectively contribute to the overall quality and stability of a relationship. Secure attachment provides a foundation for building intimacy, as individuals feel safe and supported in their emotional connections. Intimacy, in turn, reinforces commitment by deepening the emotional bond and creating a sense of shared purpose.

In contrast, insecure attachment styles can hinder the development of intimacy and commitment. For example, anxious-preoccupied individuals may struggle with trust and fear of abandonment, making it difficult to establish deep intimacy and consistent commitment. Avoidant individuals may prioritize independence over emotional closeness, leading to challenges in maintaining intimacy and long-term commitment.

The Role of Love Styles

Psychologist John Lee proposed the concept of love styles, which describes different ways individuals experience and express romantic love. Understanding these styles can provide further insights into the psychological dimensions of romantic relationships:

1. Eros: Passionate, intense love characterized by physical attraction and emotional intensity. Eros lovers prioritize romance and often seek deep, immediate connections.

2. Ludus: Playful, game-like love that values fun and excitement. Ludus lovers may avoid commitment and view love as a series of enjoyable adventures.

3. Storge: Companionate love based on friendship and shared values. Storge lovers prioritize stability, trust, and long-term partnership.

4. Pragma: Practical, pragmatic love that emphasizes compatibility and shared goals. Pragma lovers approach relationships with a focus on long-term potential and practical considerations.

5. Mania: Obsessive, intense love characterized by emotional highs and lows. Mania lovers may experience

jealousy and possessiveness, leading to turbulent relationships.

6. Agape: Selfless, altruistic love that prioritizes the well-being of the partner. Agape lovers demonstrate unconditional care and support, often putting their partner's needs above their own.

Conclusion

The psychological dimensions of romantic love—attachment, intimacy, and commitment—offer a comprehensive understanding of how love operates within human relationships. By examining these components, we can gain insights into the complexities and dynamics of romantic love, from the foundational bonds of attachment to the deep connections of intimacy and the enduring choice of commitment.

Understanding these psychological elements not only enhances our knowledge of romantic love but also provides practical insights for improving and sustaining relationships. By fostering secure attachment, cultivating intimacy, and reinforcing commitment, individuals can build strong, fulfilling, and lasting romantic partnerships.

As we continue our exploration in this book, we will delve into the chemistry of love, uncovering the neurobiological processes that drive romantic attraction and bonding. Through this journey, we aim to uncover the many layers that contribute to our experience of love and connection, enriching our understanding of this powerful and transformative force in human life.

Psychological Dimensions of Romantic Love

While evolutionary biology provides insights into the origins and adaptive functions of romantic love, psychology offers a detailed understanding of how love operates within the human mind. Psychological theories explore the components of romantic love—attachment, intimacy, and commitment—and how these elements interact to shape our relationships. By examining these dimensions, we can gain a deeper understanding of the complexities and dynamics of romantic love.

Attachment: The Foundation of Romantic Bonds

Attachment theory, developed by John Bowlby and later expanded by Mary Ainsworth, provides a framework for understanding the emotional bonds that form between romantic partners. Originally formulated to explain the bond between infants and their caregivers, attachment theory has been adapted to explore adult romantic relationships.

Types of Attachment

Attachment styles, formed during early childhood, significantly influence how individuals approach romantic relationships. There are four primary attachment styles:

1. Secure Attachment: Individuals with secure attachment styles tend to have healthy, trusting relationships. They are comfortable with intimacy and independence, and they exhibit confidence in their partner's love and support.

2. Anxious-Preoccupied Attachment: Those with an anxious-preoccupied attachment style often seek high levels of intimacy, approval, and responsiveness from their partners. They may be overly dependent on their partner and experience intense fear of abandonment.

3. Dismissive-Avoidant Attachment: Individuals with a dismissive-avoidant attachment style prioritize independence and self-reliance. They may avoid emotional closeness and have difficulty depending on others, often leading to emotional distance in relationships.

4. Fearful-Avoidant Attachment: This attachment style, also known as disorganized attachment, is characterized by a combination of fear and desire for intimacy. Individuals may have a history of trauma or inconsistent caregiving, leading to unpredictable and often turbulent relationships.

Influence on Romantic Relationships

Attachment styles profoundly affect how individuals perceive and behave in romantic relationships. Securely attached individuals are more likely to experience stable and fulfilling relationships, characterized by mutual trust, effective communication, and emotional support. In contrast, those with insecure attachment styles (anxious, avoidant, or fearful) may struggle with relationship stability and satisfaction, often experiencing cycles of conflict and distress.

Intimacy: The Emotional Connection

Intimacy is a core component of romantic love, encompassing the emotional closeness and deep connection that partners share. Psychologist Robert Sternberg, in his Triangular Theory of Love, identifies intimacy as one of the three primary components of love, alongside passion and commitment.

Building Intimacy

Intimacy involves several key elements:

1. Emotional Sharing: Partners in intimate relationships openly share their thoughts, feelings, and experiences. This emotional transparency fosters a sense of understanding and closeness.

2. Vulnerability: Intimacy requires a willingness to be vulnerable with one another. By revealing their true selves,

including fears and insecurities, partners build trust and deepen their connection.

3. Mutual Respect: Respecting each other's individuality and boundaries is essential for maintaining intimacy. This respect allows partners to feel valued and supported.

4. Quality Time: Spending meaningful time together strengthens the emotional bond between partners. Engaging in shared activities and creating memories enhances intimacy.

Challenges to Intimacy

Despite its importance, maintaining intimacy can be challenging. Life stressors, communication barriers, and unresolved conflicts can erode emotional closeness. Additionally, individuals with insecure attachment styles may find it difficult to establish and sustain intimate connections. Addressing these challenges through effective communication, empathy, and mutual effort is crucial for preserving intimacy in romantic relationships.

Commitment: The Decision to Love

Commitment represents the decision to maintain and nurture a romantic relationship over time. It involves a conscious choice to invest in the partnership, work through difficulties, and plan for a shared future. Sternberg's

Triangular Theory of Love highlights commitment as a crucial component of enduring love.

Factors Influencing Commitment

Several factors contribute to the level of commitment in a relationship:

1. Satisfaction: Relationship satisfaction, including emotional fulfillment, sexual satisfaction, and compatibility, influences commitment. Partners who are satisfied with their relationship are more likely to remain committed.

2. Investment: The time, energy, and resources invested in the relationship play a significant role in commitment. The more partners invest, the more likely they are to stay committed.

3. Alternatives: Perceptions of available alternatives impact commitment. If individuals believe they have better romantic options outside their current relationship, their commitment may wane.

4. Social and Cultural Influences: Societal norms, cultural values, and social support systems can reinforce or challenge commitment. For example, cultures that emphasize the importance of marriage and family may foster stronger commitment in relationships.

Commitment and Relationship Stability

Commitment is a key predictor of relationship stability and longevity. High levels of commitment encourage partners to work through conflicts, support each other through challenges, and prioritize the relationship's well-being. Conversely, low commitment can lead to relationship instability, increased conflict, and a higher likelihood of dissolution.

The Interaction of Attachment, Intimacy, and Commitment

The components of romantic love—attachment, intimacy, and commitment—are interrelated and collectively contribute to the overall quality and stability of a relationship. Secure attachment provides a foundation for building intimacy, as individuals feel safe and supported in their emotional connections. Intimacy, in turn, reinforces commitment by deepening the emotional bond and creating a sense of shared purpose.

In contrast, insecure attachment styles can hinder the development of intimacy and commitment. For example, anxious-preoccupied individuals may struggle with trust and fear of abandonment, making it difficult to establish deep intimacy and consistent commitment. Avoidant individuals may prioritize independence over emotional closeness, leading to challenges in maintaining intimacy and long-term commitment.

The Role of Love Styles

Psychologist John Lee proposed the concept of love styles, which describes different ways individuals experience and express romantic love. Understanding these styles can provide further insights into the psychological dimensions of romantic relationships:

1. Eros: Passionate, intense love characterized by physical attraction and emotional intensity. Eros lovers prioritize romance and often seek deep, immediate connections.

2. Ludus: Playful, game-like love that values fun and excitement. Ludus lovers may avoid commitment and view love as a series of enjoyable adventures.

3. Storge: Companionate love based on friendship and shared values. Storge lovers prioritize stability, trust, and long-term partnership.

4. Pragma: Practical, pragmatic love that emphasizes compatibility and shared goals. Pragma lovers approach relationships with a focus on long-term potential and practical considerations.

5. Mania: Obsessive, intense love characterized by emotional highs and lows. Mania lovers may experience

jealousy and possessiveness, leading to turbulent relationships.

6. Agape: Selfless, altruistic love that prioritizes the well-being of the partner. Agape lovers demonstrate unconditional care and support, often putting their partner's needs above their own.

The psychological dimensions of romantic love—attachment, intimacy, and commitment—offer a comprehensive understanding of how love operates within human relationships. By examining these components, we can gain insights into the complexities and dynamics of romantic love, from the foundational bonds of attachment to the deep connections of intimacy and the enduring choice of commitment.

Understanding these psychological elements not only enhances our knowledge of romantic love but also provides practical insights for improving and sustaining relationships. By fostering secure attachment, cultivating intimacy, and reinforcing commitment, individuals can build strong, fulfilling, and lasting romantic partnerships.

As we continue our exploration in this book, we will delve into the chemistry of love, uncovering the neurobiological processes that drive romantic attraction and bonding. Through this journey, we aim to uncover the many layers that contribute to our experience of love and connection, enriching our understanding of this powerful and transformative force in human life.

THE CHEMISTRY OF LOVE

Romantic love is not just an abstract feeling or a psychological state; it is deeply rooted in our biology. The experience of love is driven by complex neurochemical processes that influence our emotions, behaviors, and connections with others. In this chapter, we will explore the neurochemistry behind romantic love, focusing on the roles of dopamine, oxytocin, and serotonin. Understanding these neurochemicals provides insights into the powerful forces that drive attraction, attachment, and bonding in romantic relationships.

Dopamine: The Pleasure and Reward System

Dopamine is a neurotransmitter that plays a central role in the brain's reward system. It is associated with pleasure, motivation, and the reinforcement of rewarding behaviors.

When we experience romantic attraction, dopamine levels increase, creating feelings of euphoria and excitement.

The Role of Dopamine in Romantic Love

1. Attraction and Desire: Dopamine is crucial in the initial stages of romantic attraction. When we are attracted to someone, our brain releases dopamine, which creates a sense of anticipation and desire. This neurochemical response motivates us to pursue the object of our affection, enhancing our focus and energy.

2. Pleasure and Reward: The presence of a romantic partner activates the brain's reward circuitry. Positive interactions, such as physical touch, affectionate gestures, and intimate conversations, lead to dopamine release, reinforcing the pleasurable experience of being in love. This reward mechanism encourages us to seek repeated interactions with our partner, strengthening the romantic bond.

3. Risk-Taking and Novelty: Dopamine is also linked to risk-taking behavior and the pursuit of novelty. In the context of romantic love, this can manifest as the willingness to take emotional risks, such as expressing vulnerability or making long-term commitments. The excitement of new experiences and the novelty of a budding romance are fueled by dopamine, making the early stages of love particularly exhilarating.

Oxytocin: The Bonding Hormone

Oxytocin, often referred to as the "love hormone," is a neuropeptide that plays a crucial role in social bonding, trust, and attachment. It is released during physical touch, sexual activity, and childbirth, promoting feelings of closeness and connection between individuals.

The Role of Oxytocin in Romantic Love

1. Physical Touch and Intimacy: Oxytocin is released in response to physical touch, such as hugging, kissing, and sexual activity. This release fosters a sense of intimacy and emotional closeness, strengthening the bond between romantic partners. The comforting and soothing effects of oxytocin contribute to the feeling of being "in sync" with a partner.

2. Trust and Empathy: Oxytocin enhances trust and empathy, which are essential components of a healthy romantic relationship. Higher levels of oxytocin are associated with increased trust in others and the ability to empathize with a partner's emotions and experiences. This neurochemical support for trust and empathy facilitates deeper emotional connections and effective communication.

3. Attachment and Bonding: Oxytocin is instrumental in the formation and maintenance of long-term attachments. It promotes a sense of security and stability in relationships,

encouraging partners to remain committed and supportive of one another. The hormone's role in attachment is evident in the strong emotional bonds formed between parents and children, as well as between romantic partners.

Serotonin: The Mood Stabilizer

Serotonin is a neurotransmitter that helps regulate mood, anxiety, and overall emotional stability. While its role in romantic love is less direct than that of dopamine and oxytocin, serotonin significantly influences our emotional well-being and relationship satisfaction.

The Role of Serotonin in Romantic Love

1. Mood Regulation: Serotonin levels are closely linked to mood regulation. Adequate serotonin levels contribute to feelings of happiness, contentment, and emotional stability. In the context of romantic love, stable serotonin levels help maintain a positive mood, reducing the likelihood of conflicts and negative interactions.

2. Obsessive Thoughts and Behavior: Interestingly, low levels of serotonin are associated with obsessive thoughts and behaviors, which can manifest in the early stages of romantic love as infatuation. This intense focus on a romantic partner, driven by reduced serotonin, can lead to heightened attention and preoccupation with the relationship.

3. Relationship Satisfaction: Serotonin also plays a role in overall relationship satisfaction. Balanced serotonin levels contribute to emotional resilience and the ability to cope with relationship stressors. Partners with stable serotonin levels are more likely to experience harmonious and satisfying relationships.

The Interplay of Neurochemicals in Romantic Love

The experience of romantic love is not driven by a single neurochemical but rather by the interplay of dopamine, oxytocin, and serotonin. Each of these neurochemicals contributes to different aspects of love, from the initial spark of attraction to the deep bonds of long-term attachment.

Phases of Romantic Love

1. Lust and Attraction: The initial phase of romantic love, characterized by lust and attraction, is dominated by dopamine and, to some extent, by low serotonin levels. This phase involves intense desire, excitement, and infatuation, driven by the brain's reward system.

2. Romantic Love: As the relationship progresses, oxytocin plays a more prominent role. This phase is marked by increasing intimacy, trust, and emotional bonding. The release of oxytocin during physical touch and intimate interactions strengthens the attachment between partners.

3. Attachment: In long-term relationships, serotonin contributes to emotional stability and relationship satisfaction. The ongoing presence of oxytocin supports attachment and bonding, while balanced serotonin levels help maintain a positive mood and emotional resilience.

Factors Influencing Neurochemical Responses

Several factors can influence the neurochemical responses associated with romantic love, including individual differences, relationship dynamics, and external stressors.

1. Individual Differences: Genetic and personality differences can affect how individuals experience and respond to romantic love. For example, variations in dopamine receptor genes may influence susceptibility to romantic attraction and risk-taking behaviors.

2. Relationship Dynamics: The quality of the relationship itself can impact neurochemical responses. Positive interactions, effective communication, and mutual support can enhance dopamine and oxytocin release, reinforcing the bond between partners.

3. External Stressors: External stressors, such as work pressures, financial difficulties, or health issues, can affect neurochemical balance and relationship dynamics. Chronic stress can reduce dopamine and serotonin levels, leading to decreased relationship satisfaction and increased conflict.

The neurochemistry of romantic love reveals the intricate biological processes that underpin our emotional experiences and connections with others. Dopamine drives attraction and desire, oxytocin fosters bonding and intimacy, and serotonin stabilizes mood and enhances relationship satisfaction. Together, these neurochemicals create the rich tapestry of emotions that define romantic love.

Understanding the neurochemical basis of love provides valuable insights into the nature of human relationships and the factors that contribute to their success and stability. By recognizing the biological underpinnings of love, we can better navigate the complexities of romantic relationships, fostering deeper connections and greater emotional fulfillment.

As we continue our exploration in this book, we will delve into the spiritual dimensions of love, examining how faith, spirituality, and personal growth intersect with our experience of romantic love. Through this journey, we aim to uncover the many layers that contribute to our understanding of love, enriching our appreciation of this powerful and transformative force in human life.

The Chemistry of Love

Romantic love is not just an abstract feeling or a psychological state; it is deeply rooted in our biology. The experience of love is driven by complex neurochemical processes that influence our emotions, behaviors, and connections with others. In this chapter, we will explore the role of hormones in romantic love, focusing on their involvement in attraction, bonding, and long-term relationships. Understanding these hormones provides insights into the powerful forces that drive our romantic experiences and sustain our relationships over time.

The Role of Hormones in Attraction

The initial phase of romantic love, characterized by attraction and desire, is heavily influenced by hormones that create intense feelings of excitement and anticipation. The primary hormones involved in this stage are dopamine, testosterone, and norepinephrine.

Dopamine: The Pleasure and Reward System

Dopamine is a neurotransmitter that plays a central role in the brain's reward system. It is associated with pleasure, motivation, and the reinforcement of rewarding behaviors. When we experience romantic attraction, dopamine levels increase, creating feelings of euphoria and excitement.

1. Attraction and Desire: Dopamine is crucial in the initial stages of romantic attraction. When we are attracted to someone, our brain releases dopamine, which creates a sense of anticipation and desire. This neurochemical response

motivates us to pursue the object of our affection, enhancing our focus and energy.

2. Pleasure and Reward: The presence of a romantic partner activates the brain's reward circuitry. Positive interactions, such as physical touch, affectionate gestures, and intimate conversations, lead to dopamine release, reinforcing the pleasurable experience of being in love. This reward mechanism encourages us to seek repeated interactions with our partner, strengthening the romantic bond.

Testosterone: The Hormone of Desire

Testosterone is often associated with male sexuality, but it plays a significant role in the romantic attraction of both men and women. It influences sexual desire, competitive behaviors, and the pursuit of romantic partners.

1. Sexual Desire: Elevated levels of testosterone increase sexual desire and drive, making individuals more motivated to seek romantic and sexual encounters. This heightened desire is a key component of the attraction phase, fostering the pursuit of potential mates.

2. Confidence and Risk-Taking: Testosterone also boosts confidence and willingness to take risks, which can be advantageous in the context of romantic pursuits. Individuals with higher testosterone levels may exhibit more assertive and competitive behaviors in the quest for a romantic partner.

Norepinephrine: The Excitement Hormone

Norepinephrine, also known as noradrenaline, is a hormone and neurotransmitter that plays a role in the body's "fight-or-flight" response. It is associated with heightened arousal, alertness, and energy.

1. Arousal and Excitement: During the attraction phase, norepinephrine levels rise, leading to increased arousal and excitement. This hormone contributes to the physical sensations of a racing heart, sweaty palms, and butterflies in the stomach that often accompany romantic attraction.

2. Focus and Attention: Norepinephrine enhances focus and attention, making individuals more attuned to their romantic interest. This heightened awareness allows for greater responsiveness to the partner's needs and behaviors, facilitating the development of a romantic connection.

The Role of Hormones in Bonding

As romantic relationships progress, hormones that promote bonding and emotional attachment become more prominent. Oxytocin and vasopressin are the primary hormones involved in creating and sustaining these bonds.

Oxytocin: The Bonding Hormone

Oxytocin, often referred to as the "love hormone," is a neuropeptide that plays a crucial role in social bonding, trust, and attachment. It is released during physical touch, sexual activity, and childbirth, promoting feelings of closeness and connection between individuals.

1. Physical Touch and Intimacy: Oxytocin is released in response to physical touch, such as hugging, kissing, and sexual activity. This release fosters a sense of intimacy and emotional closeness, strengthening the bond between romantic partners. The comforting and soothing effects of oxytocin contribute to the feeling of being "in sync" with a partner.

2. Trust and Empathy: Oxytocin enhances trust and empathy, which are essential components of a healthy romantic relationship. Higher levels of oxytocin are associated with increased trust in others and the ability to empathize with a partner's emotions and experiences. This neurochemical support for trust and empathy facilitates deeper emotional connections and effective communication.

3. Attachment and Bonding: Oxytocin is instrumental in the formation and maintenance of long-term attachments. It promotes a sense of security and stability in relationships, encouraging partners to remain committed and supportive of one another. The hormone's role in attachment is evident in the strong emotional bonds formed between parents and children, as well as between romantic partners.

Vasopressin: The Monogamy Hormone

Vasopressin is another hormone that plays a significant role in social behavior and bonding, particularly in promoting monogamous relationships and long-term commitment.

1. Monogamy and Mate Guarding: Research on prairie voles, a monogamous species, has shown that vasopressin is linked to pair bonding and mate guarding behaviors. In humans, higher levels of vasopressin are associated with an increased likelihood of monogamous relationships and long-term commitment.

2. Protective Behaviors: Vasopressin encourages protective behaviors toward a partner, fostering a sense of loyalty and commitment. This hormone's influence on mate guarding helps maintain the exclusivity of the romantic relationship, reducing the likelihood of infidelity.

The Role of Hormones in Long-Term Relationships

Sustaining a long-term romantic relationship involves a balance of hormones that support emotional stability, satisfaction, and resilience. Serotonin and endorphins play crucial roles in maintaining these aspects of long-term love.

Serotonin: The Mood Stabilizer

Serotonin is a neurotransmitter that helps regulate mood, anxiety, and overall emotional stability. While its role in romantic love is less direct than that of dopamine and oxytocin, serotonin significantly influences our emotional well-being and relationship satisfaction.

1. Mood Regulation: Serotonin levels are closely linked to mood regulation. Adequate serotonin levels contribute to feelings of happiness, contentment, and emotional stability. In the context of romantic love, stable serotonin levels help maintain a positive mood, reducing the likelihood of conflicts and negative interactions.

2. Obsessive Thoughts and Behavior: Interestingly, low levels of serotonin are associated with obsessive thoughts and behaviors, which can manifest in the early stages of romantic love as infatuation. This intense focus on a romantic partner, driven by reduced serotonin, can lead to heightened attention and preoccupation with the relationship.

3. Relationship Satisfaction: Serotonin also plays a role in overall relationship satisfaction. Balanced serotonin levels contribute to emotional resilience and the ability to cope with relationship stressors. Partners with stable serotonin levels are more likely to experience harmonious and satisfying relationships.

Endorphins: The Natural Painkillers

Endorphins are neurotransmitters that act as natural painkillers and mood enhancers. They are released during physical activity, laughter, and other pleasurable activities.

1. Emotional Bonding: Endorphins promote a sense of well-being and happiness, which can strengthen emotional bonds between partners. The release of endorphins during shared activities, such as exercising or laughing together, enhances the overall positive experience of the relationship.

2. Stress Reduction: Endorphins help reduce stress and anxiety, contributing to emotional stability in long-term relationships. By mitigating the impact of external stressors, endorphins support a positive and resilient relationship dynamic.

The Interplay of Hormones in Romantic Relationships

The experience of romantic love is not driven by a single hormone but rather by the interplay of multiple hormones that influence different aspects of the relationship. Each hormone contributes to different phases of love, from the initial attraction to long-term bonding and stability.

Phases of Romantic Love

1. Lust and Attraction: The initial phase of romantic love, characterized by lust and attraction, is dominated by dopamine, testosterone, and norepinephrine. This phase involves intense desire, excitement, and infatuation, driven by the brain's reward system.

2. Romantic Love: As the relationship progresses, oxytocin and vasopressin play more prominent roles. This phase is marked by increasing intimacy, trust, and emotional bonding. The release of oxytocin during physical touch and intimate interactions strengthens the attachment between partners, while vasopressin promotes commitment and monogamy.

3. Attachment: In long-term relationships, serotonin and endorphins contribute to emotional stability and relationship satisfaction. The ongoing presence of oxytocin and vasopressin supports attachment and bonding, while balanced serotonin levels help maintain a positive mood and emotional resilience. Endorphins enhance the overall well-being of the partners, reducing stress and fostering a sense of happiness.

Factors Influencing Hormonal Responses

Several factors can influence the hormonal responses associated with romantic love, including individual differences, relationship dynamics, and external stressors.

1. Individual Differences: Genetic and personality differences can affect how individuals experience and respond to romantic love. For example, variations in dopamine receptor genes may influence susceptibility to romantic attraction and risk-taking behaviors.

2. Relationship Dynamics: The quality of the relationship itself can impact hormonal responses. Positive interactions, effective communication, and mutual support can enhance dopamine and oxytocin release, reinforcing the bond between partners.

3. External Stressors: External stressors, such as work pressures, financial difficulties, or health issues, can affect hormonal balance and relationship dynamics. Chronic stress can reduce dopamine and serotonin levels, leading to decreased relationship satisfaction and increased conflict.

The chemistry of romantic love reveals the intricate biological processes that underpin our emotional experiences and connections with others. Dopamine drives attraction and desire, oxytocin and vasopressin foster bonding and commitment, and serotonin and endorphins maintain emotional stability and satisfaction. Together, these hormones create the rich tapestry of emotions that define romantic love.

Understanding the hormonal basis of love provides valuable insights into the nature of human relationships and the factors that contribute to their success and stability. By recognizing the biological underpinnings of love, we can better navigate the complexities of romantic relationships, fostering deeper connections and greater emotional fulfillment.

As we continue our exploration in this book, we will delve into the spiritual dimensions of love, examining how faith, spirituality, and personal growth intersect with our experience of romantic love. Through this journey, we aim to uncover the many layers that contribute to our understanding of love, enriching our appreciation of this powerful and transformative force in human life.

CHAPTER 04

CULTURAL AND SOCIETAL INFLUENCES ON ROMANTIC LOVE

Romantic love, while deeply rooted in biological and psychological processes, does not exist in a vacuum. Cultural norms and societal expectations play a significant role in shaping how individuals experience and express love. These cultural and societal influences affect everything from mate selection and courtship practices to relationship dynamics and the concept of marriage. In this chapter, we will investigate how cultural norms and societal expectations shape romantic relationships, highlighting the diversity of romantic love across different societies and historical periods.

Cultural Variations in Mate Selection

Different cultures have diverse criteria for mate selection, reflecting societal values and priorities. These criteria can influence the importance placed on attributes such as physical appearance, social status, education, and family background.

1. Arranged Marriages: In many cultures, arranged marriages are a common practice. Families play a central role in choosing partners based on social status, economic stability, and compatibility. The emphasis is often on long-term stability and the well-being of the extended family rather than individual romantic desire.

2. Love Marriages: In contrast, cultures that prioritize individualism often emphasize personal choice and romantic attraction in mate selection. Love marriages, where individuals choose their partners based on mutual affection and emotional connection, are more common in these societies.

3. Hybrid Approaches: Some cultures adopt a hybrid approach, where individuals have a say in the selection process, but family approval remains important. This blend of personal choice and family involvement reflects a balance between individual desires and societal expectations.

Courtship Practices and Rituals

Courtship practices and rituals vary widely across cultures, shaping how romantic relationships develop and are formalized. These practices often reflect cultural values and traditions.

1. Formal Courtship: In some cultures, courtship follows formalized rituals and procedures. These may include chaperoned meetings, exchange of gifts, and adherence to strict social norms. Formal courtship practices emphasize propriety, respect, and the gradual development of a relationship.

2. Casual Dating: In cultures with more liberal attitudes toward romantic relationships, casual dating is common. Individuals have the freedom to meet and interact in various social settings, allowing for spontaneous connections and the exploration of multiple relationships before committing to one partner.

3. Online Dating: The advent of technology has transformed courtship practices globally. Online dating platforms provide new avenues for meeting potential partners, and transcending geographical and cultural boundaries. This shift has introduced new dynamics in mate selection and relationship development.

Gender Roles and Power Dynamics

Cultural norms and societal expectations heavily influence gender roles and power dynamics within romantic relationships. These roles can affect communication, decision-making, and the division of responsibilities.

1. Traditional Gender Roles: In many cultures, traditional gender roles prescribe specific behaviors and expectations for men and women. Men are often expected to be providers and protectors, while women are seen as caregivers and homemakers. These roles can create power imbalances and affect the distribution of authority within a relationship.

2. Evolving Gender Roles: As societies evolve, gender roles are increasingly challenged and redefined. Greater emphasis on gender equality and empowerment allows for more balanced relationships, where both partners share responsibilities and decision-making. This shift promotes mutual respect and collaboration.

3. Intersectionality: Gender roles intersect with other aspects of identity, such as race, class, and sexual orientation. Understanding these intersections is crucial for appreciating the diverse experiences of romantic love and addressing the unique challenges faced by different groups.

Marriage and Family Structures

Marriage and family structures vary across cultures, reflecting different attitudes toward romantic love and partnership. These structures influence the formation, maintenance, and dissolution of romantic relationships.

1. Monogamy and Polygamy: Monogamy, the practice of having one partner at a time, is the most common marital structure worldwide. However, polygamy, where an individual has multiple spouses, is practiced in some cultures. These differing structures reflect cultural norms and legal frameworks governing relationships.

2. Nuclear and Extended Families: In many Western cultures, the nuclear family—comprising two parents and their children—is the dominant family structure. In contrast, extended families, including multiple generations and relatives living together, are more common in other parts of the world. The family structure influences the roles and responsibilities within romantic relationships.

3. Same-Sex Marriage: Legal recognition of same-sex marriage varies globally. In some countries, same-sex couples have the right to marry and enjoy legal protections, while in others, such relationships are not recognized or are criminalized. Societal attitudes toward same-sex marriage reflect broader cultural and legal contexts.

Cultural Expressions of Love

Cultural expressions of love, such as language, art, literature, and rituals, shape how individuals experience and communicate romantic love. These expressions provide insight into the values and emotions associated with love in different cultures.

1. Language of Love: Different cultures have unique ways of expressing love through language. Some languages have multiple words for different types of love, capturing the nuances of romantic, familial, and platonic affection. These linguistic variations reflect cultural understandings of love.

2. Art and Literature: Art and literature serve as powerful mediums for expressing and exploring romantic love. Cultural artifacts, such as poetry, music, and visual art, provide rich narratives of love, passion, and heartbreak. These works influence and reflect societal attitudes toward love.

3. Rituals and Traditions: Cultural rituals and traditions surrounding love and marriage highlight the significance of romantic relationships. Wedding ceremonies, anniversaries, and other celebrations serve to formalize and reinforce romantic bonds. These rituals often involve symbolic acts that express commitment and unity.

Impact of Globalization on Romantic Love

Globalization has facilitated the exchange of cultural ideas and practices, influencing how romantic love is experienced and expressed worldwide. This exchange has led to the blending of traditions and the emergence of new relationship dynamics.

1. Cultural Convergence: Exposure to different cultural norms and practices through media, travel, and migration can lead to the convergence of relationship behaviors. Individuals may adopt practices from other cultures, creating hybrid forms of romantic expression.

2. Cultural Resistance: While globalization promotes cultural exchange, it can also lead to resistance and the reaffirmation of traditional values. Some societies may seek to preserve their unique cultural identity by emphasizing traditional courtship and marriage practices.

3. Intercultural Relationships: Globalization has increased the prevalence of intercultural relationships, where partners from different cultural backgrounds navigate and blend their distinct traditions and values. These relationships offer opportunities for cross-cultural understanding and enrichment.

Cultural norms and societal expectations play a pivotal role in shaping romantic relationships. From mate selection and courtship practices to gender roles and family structures, these influences create a rich tapestry of romantic experiences across different societies. Understanding the cultural and societal context of romantic love allows us to appreciate its diversity and complexity.

As we continue our exploration in this book, we will delve into the spiritual dimensions of love, examining how faith, spirituality, and personal growth intersect with our experience of romantic love. Through this journey, we aim to uncover the many layers that contribute to our understanding of love, enriching our appreciation of this powerful and transformative force in human life.

Cultural and Societal Influences on Romantic Love

Romantic love, while deeply rooted in biological and psychological processes, does not exist in a vacuum. Cultural norms and societal expectations play a significant role in shaping how individuals experience and express love. These cultural and societal influences affect everything from mate selection and courtship practices to relationship dynamics and the concept of marriage. In this chapter, we will investigate how media, literature, and social media influence modern concepts of romantic love, highlighting the profound impact these forces have on shaping our romantic ideals and behaviors.

The Role of Media in Shaping Romantic Love

Media, including television, movies, and music, plays a significant role in shaping societal perceptions of romantic love. The portrayal of romantic relationships in media can influence our expectations, desires, and behaviors in profound ways.

Television and Movies

1. Idealized Relationships: Television shows and movies often depict idealized versions of romantic relationships, where love conquers all obstacles, and partners are perfectly compatible. These portrayals can create unrealistic expectations about what romantic relationships should be like, leading to disappointment and dissatisfaction when real-life relationships fail to measure up.

2. Stereotypes and Tropes: Media frequently relies on stereotypes and tropes to tell romantic stories. Common tropes include the "happily ever after" ending, the "love at first sight" phenomenon, and the "knight in shining armor" rescuing the damsel in distress. While these narratives can be entertaining, they often reinforce traditional gender roles and narrow definitions of love.

3. Diverse Representations: In recent years, there has been a push for more diverse and inclusive representations of romantic love in media. Shows and movies featuring LGBTQ+ relationships, interracial couples, and non-

traditional family structures challenge the dominant narratives and offer a broader view of what love can look like.

Music and Romantic Love

1. Emotional Expression: Music is a powerful medium for expressing the emotions associated with romantic love. Love songs often capture the joy, longing, heartache, and passion of romantic relationships, resonating deeply with listeners and shaping their emotional experiences.

2. Cultural Influence: Different genres of music reflect cultural attitudes toward love and relationships. For example, country music might emphasize traditional values and enduring love, while pop music often focuses on the excitement and intensity of new love. These cultural influences shape how individuals perceive and experience romantic love.

3. Impact on Behavior: The themes and messages in romantic music can influence relationship behaviors. For instance, songs that glorify possessiveness or infidelity might normalize such behaviors, while songs that celebrate mutual respect and commitment can reinforce positive relationship values.

The Influence of Literature on Romantic Love

Literature has long been a source of inspiration and reflection on romantic love. From classic novels to contemporary romance fiction, literature shapes our understanding of love and relationships.

Classic Romantic Literature

1. Enduring Themes: Classic romantic literature, such as the works of Jane Austen, Emily Brontë, and Leo Tolstoy, explores timeless themes of love, passion, and heartache. These stories often highlight the complexities of romantic relationships, including societal constraints, personal sacrifices, and moral dilemmas.

2. Cultural Impact: The themes and characters in classic romantic literature have had a lasting impact on cultural perceptions of love. For example, the enduring appeal of Elizabeth Bennet and Mr. Darcy from "Pride and Prejudice" continues to influence modern romantic ideals and expectations.

Contemporary Romance Fiction

1. Diverse Narratives: Contemporary romance fiction encompasses a wide range of narratives, from light-hearted romantic comedies to emotionally intense dramas. This diversity reflects the varied experiences of love in the modern world, offering readers multiple perspectives on romantic relationships.

2. Empowerment and Agency: Many contemporary romance novels emphasize the empowerment and agency of

their protagonists, particularly female characters. These stories often highlight themes of personal growth, self-discovery, and mutual respect in relationships, challenging traditional gender roles and expectations.

3. Escapism and Fantasy: Romance fiction provides an escape from the challenges of everyday life, allowing readers to immerse themselves in idealized worlds where love triumphs over adversity. While this escapism can be enjoyable, it is important to recognize the difference between fictional romantic fantasies and real-life relationships.

The Impact of Social Media on Romantic Love

Social media has revolutionized the way we experience and express romantic love. Platforms like Facebook, Instagram, and Tinder have created new dynamics in how we connect with others, share our relationships, and navigate romantic experiences.

Online Dating and Connectivity

1. Access to Potential Partners: Online dating platforms have expanded the pool of potential romantic partners, allowing individuals to connect with others beyond their immediate social circles. This increased access can lead to more opportunities for finding compatible partners and exploring diverse relationship experiences.

2. Personal Branding: Social media profiles act as a form of personal branding, where individuals curate their online presence to attract potential partners. This curation can involve highlighting attractive qualities, interests, and experiences, shaping how others perceive and approach them.

3. Instant Communication: The ability to communicate instantly through messaging apps and social media platforms has transformed the pace and nature of romantic interactions. While this connectivity can facilitate closeness and intimacy, it can also create challenges such as misunderstandings and the pressure to be constantly available.

The Public Display of Relationships

1. Relationship Validation: Social media allows individuals to publicly display their romantic relationships through posts, photos, and status updates. This public validation can reinforce the relationship and provide a sense of community support, but it can also create pressure to present a perfect image of the relationship.

2. Comparison and Envy: Constant exposure to curated images of other people's relationships can lead to comparison and envy. Individuals may feel inadequate or dissatisfied with their own relationships when they compare them to the seemingly perfect relationships displayed on social media.

3. Digital Intimacy: Social media can facilitate digital intimacy through private messages, shared experiences, and virtual expressions of affection. However, the lack of face-to-face interaction can also lead to challenges in building deep emotional connections and understanding non-verbal cues.

Influence on Relationship Dynamics

1. Transparency and Trust: Social media can enhance transparency and trust in relationships by allowing partners to stay connected and share their lives. However, it can also create issues related to privacy and boundaries, leading to potential conflicts over social media use and online interactions.

2. Conflict and Resolution: Social media can exacerbate conflicts in relationships, as misunderstandings and disagreements can be amplified in the digital space. On the other hand, it can also provide tools for resolving conflicts, such as communication platforms and relationship advice resources.

3. Impact on Breakups: The presence of social media can complicate the process of breaking up. The visibility of an ex-partner's life, mutual friends, and shared memories can make it difficult to move on. Some individuals may choose to unfollow or block their ex-partners to facilitate emotional healing.

Media, literature, and social media have a profound impact on modern concepts of romantic love. They shape our expectations, desires, and behaviors in romantic relationships, influencing how we connect with others and navigate the complexities of love. While these cultural and societal influences can provide valuable insights and inspiration, it is important to approach them critically and recognize the difference between idealized portrayals and real-life experiences.

As we continue our exploration in this book, we will delve into the spiritual dimensions of love, examining how faith, spirituality, and personal growth intersect with our experience of romantic love. Through this journey, we aim to uncover the many layers that contribute to our understanding of love, enriching our appreciation of this powerful and transformative force in human life.

CHAPTER 05

SPIRITUAL DIMENSIONS OF LOVE

Romantic love is not only a biological and psychological phenomenon but also a deeply spiritual experience. Across various religions and belief systems, love is often seen as a divine force that transcends the physical and emotional realms. This chapter explores the spiritual dimensions of love, examining how different religions and belief systems understand and experience romantic love. By delving into these spiritual aspects, we gain a richer and more comprehensive understanding of love's profound impact on human life.

Christianity: Love as Divine and Sacred

In Christianity, love is considered one of the highest virtues and a reflection of God's nature. The Bible emphasizes love as a fundamental principle, both in human relationships and in the relationship between humans and God.

1. Agape Love: Agape is the Greek term for selfless, unconditional love. In Christian theology, agape love

represents God's love for humanity, characterized by self-sacrifice and compassion. This form of love is often seen in the context of romantic relationships as a model for how partners should love each other selflessly and unconditionally.

2. Marriage as a Sacred Covenant: In Christianity, marriage is viewed as a sacred covenant between two individuals and God. This covenant is meant to reflect the relationship between Christ and the Church, emphasizing mutual love, respect, and commitment. Ephesians 5:25, for example, instructs husbands to love their wives "just as Christ loved the church and gave himself up for her."

3. The Role of Prayer and Faith: Christian couples often integrate prayer and faith into their relationships, seeking divine guidance and strength to navigate challenges. The spiritual practice of praying together can foster deeper emotional and spiritual intimacy, reinforcing the bond between partners.

Islam: Love and Compassion in Relationships

Islam places a strong emphasis on love and compassion in all human relationships, including romantic ones. The teachings of the Quran and the Hadith provide guidance on how to cultivate love and maintain healthy relationships.

1. Rahmah and Mawaddah: The Quran uses the terms "rahmah" (mercy) and "mawaddah" (affection) to describe the ideal qualities of a marital relationship. Surah Ar-Rum (30:21) states, "And of His signs is that He created for you from yourselves mates that you may find tranquility in them; and He placed between you affection and mercy. Indeed, in that are signs for a people who give thought." These principles highlight the importance of compassion, kindness, and mutual support in marriage.

2. Marriage as a Sunnah: Following the Sunnah (the practices of Prophet Muhammad) is central to Islamic life. The Prophet Muhammad emphasized the importance of marriage and described it as half of one's faith. He encouraged treating one's spouse with love, kindness, and respect, setting a model for Muslim couples to follow.

3. Spiritual Practices in Marriage: Islamic spiritual practices, such as praying together, reading the Quran, and fasting during Ramadan, can strengthen the marital bond. These shared religious activities promote spiritual growth and unity, helping couples navigate life's challenges with a sense of shared purpose and faith.

Hinduism: Love as a Path to Spiritual Enlightenment

In Hinduism, love is seen as a powerful force that can lead to spiritual growth and enlightenment. The concepts of

Bhakti (devotion) and the various forms of love described in ancient texts highlight the spiritual dimensions of romantic love.

1. Bhakti and Devotion: Bhakti, or devotional love, is a key aspect of Hindu spirituality. While it primarily refers to love and devotion to a deity, the principles of Bhakti can also be applied to romantic relationships. This form of love emphasizes selflessness, dedication, and the merging of the individual soul with the divine, mirroring the deep connection that can exist between romantic partners.

2. The Kama Sutra and the Art of Love: The Kama Sutra, an ancient Hindu text, explores the art of love and relationships. While often misunderstood as purely a manual on sexual positions, the Kama Sutra also delves into the emotional and spiritual aspects of love, offering guidance on how to cultivate deep, meaningful connections between partners.

3. Marriage as a Sacred Union: Hindu marriages are considered sacred unions, often conducted through elaborate rituals and ceremonies. The seven vows (Saptapadi) taken during the wedding ceremony symbolize the couple's commitment to support each other through life's journey, fostering both worldly and spiritual growth.

Buddhism: Compassionate and Mindful Love

Buddhism emphasizes compassion, mindfulness, and the development of loving-kindness (Metta) in all relationships. These principles offer a framework for understanding and nurturing romantic love.

1. Loving-Kindness (Metta): Metta is a foundational practice in Buddhism, involving the cultivation of unconditional love and compassion for all beings. In romantic relationships, practicing Metta encourages partners to approach each other with kindness, empathy, and a desire for mutual well-being.

2. Mindfulness and Presence: Mindfulness, or the practice of being fully present in the moment, is a key aspect of Buddhist practice. In the context of romantic love, mindfulness helps partners to truly listen to each other, appreciate each moment together, and respond to each other's needs with attentiveness and care.

3. Non-Attachment and Freedom: Buddhism teaches the concept of non-attachment, which involves letting go of clinging and possessiveness. In romantic relationships, this principle encourages partners to love each other without seeking to control or possess, fostering a sense of freedom and mutual respect.

Judaism: Covenant and Commitment

In Judaism, love is viewed through the lens of covenant and commitment, with marriage being a central institution that reflects the relationship between God and the Jewish people.

1. Ahava and Chesed: The Hebrew words "ahava" (love) and "chesed" (loving-kindness) describe the ideal qualities of a romantic relationship. These concepts emphasize enduring love, kindness, and commitment, forming the foundation of a strong and supportive partnership.

2. Marriage as a Covenant: Jewish marriage (kiddushin) is considered a covenant between two individuals and God. This covenantal relationship is marked by mutual obligations, respect, and the intention to build a family and community based on Jewish values and traditions.

3. Rituals and Practices: Jewish couples often engage in rituals and practices that reinforce their spiritual bond, such as observing Shabbat together, participating in holiday celebrations, and engaging in regular study of Torah. These shared religious activities strengthen the couple's connection to each other and their faith.

Taoism: Harmony and Balance in Love

Taoism, with its focus on harmony, balance, and the flow of energy (Qi), offers unique insights into the spiritual dimensions of romantic love.

1. Yin and Yang: The Taoist concept of Yin and Yang represents the complementary forces that create balance in the universe. In romantic relationships, this principle encourages partners to embrace their differences and seek harmony, recognizing that both masculine (Yang) and feminine (Yin) energies are essential for a balanced partnership.

2. The Way (Tao) of Love: Taoism teaches that love should flow naturally, without force or manipulation. By following the Tao, or the natural way, couples can cultivate a relationship that is harmonious, spontaneous, and aligned with the natural rhythms of life.

3. Energy and Intimacy: Taoist practices, such as Tai Chi and Qigong, focus on cultivating and balancing the body's energy. In the context of romantic love, these practices can enhance intimacy and connection by promoting physical and emotional well-being.

Indigenous and Ancestral Beliefs: Love as Connection to the Earth and Community

Many Indigenous and ancestral belief systems emphasize the interconnectedness of all life and the importance of community and relationship with the natural world. These principles deeply influence their understanding of romantic love.

1. Sacred Union and Community: In many Indigenous cultures, marriage and romantic relationships are seen as sacred unions that contribute to the well-being of the community. The health and harmony of the relationship are considered vital for the prosperity of the entire community.

2. Rituals and Ceremonies: Indigenous cultures often incorporate rituals and ceremonies to honor romantic unions. These ceremonies may involve the blessing of the natural elements, the guidance of ancestors, and the participation of the community, emphasizing the spiritual significance of the partnership.

3. Connection to the Earth: Indigenous beliefs often highlight the importance of living in harmony with the Earth. In romantic relationships, this connection to nature can foster a deep sense of grounding, balance, and respect for the interconnectedness of all life.

The spiritual dimensions of love offer profound insights into the nature of romantic relationships. Across different religions and belief systems, love is seen as a divine force that transcends the physical and emotional realms, enriching our lives and guiding our relationships. By exploring these spiritual aspects, we gain a deeper understanding of love's transformative power and its role in our journey toward personal and collective growth.

As we continue our exploration in this book, we will delve into the health and psychological benefits of romantic love, examining how love impacts our well-being and mental health. Through this journey, we aim to uncover the many layers that contribute to our understanding of love, enriching our appreciation of this powerful and transformative force in human life.

Spiritual Dimensions of Love

Spirituality and faith deeply influence how individuals perceive and experience romantic love. These elements provide a framework for understanding love as a divine and transcendent force that shapes our relationships and guides our behaviors. In this chapter, we will explore how spirituality and faith impact romantic relationships, examining the ways they influence perceptions of love, relationship dynamics, and the practices that foster deeper connections between partners.

The Role of Spirituality in Romantic Relationships

Spirituality encompasses a broad range of beliefs and practices that connect individuals to something greater than themselves. It provides a sense of meaning and purpose, which can profoundly shape romantic relationships.

1. A Sense of Purpose: Spirituality often imbues relationships with a deeper sense of purpose. Partners who share spiritual beliefs may view their relationship as part of a divine plan or a journey toward personal and collective growth. This shared purpose can strengthen the bond between partners and provide a foundation for enduring love.

2. Values and Principles: Spirituality often promotes values such as compassion, forgiveness, and selflessness. These values can positively influence relationship dynamics by encouraging partners to treat each other with kindness and understanding. Spiritual principles can also guide decision-making and conflict resolution within the relationship.

3. Emotional Resilience: Spirituality can provide emotional resilience during challenging times. The belief in a higher power or a greater purpose can offer comfort and hope, helping partners navigate difficulties with a sense of faith and optimism. Spiritual practices such as prayer, meditation, and mindfulness can also reduce stress and enhance emotional well-being.

The Influence of Faith on Perceptions of Love

Faith, whether rooted in organized religion or personal beliefs, profoundly shapes how individuals perceive and experience love. Different faith traditions offer unique perspectives on the nature of love and its role in human life.

Christianity: Love as a Reflection of God's Love

1. Agape Love: In Christianity, agape love represents selfless, unconditional love. This concept influences how Christians perceive romantic love, emphasizing the importance of loving one's partner selflessly and sacrificially. The ideal of agape love encourages partners to prioritize each other's well-being and to demonstrate love through actions.

2. Marriage as a Covenant: Christians often view marriage as a sacred covenant that mirrors the relationship between Christ and the Church. This covenantal perspective emphasizes commitment, fidelity, and mutual support. The belief that marriage is divinely ordained can strengthen the resolve to work through challenges and maintain a loving partnership.

3. Spiritual Growth: Many Christians believe that romantic relationships and marriage are opportunities for spiritual growth. Through the experiences of loving, forgiving, and supporting each other, partners can deepen their faith and grow closer to God.

Islam: Compassion and Partnership

1. Compassion and Mercy (Rahmah and Mawaddah): In Islam, the Quran emphasizes the qualities of compassion (rahmah) and affection (mawaddah) in marriage. These principles encourage partners to approach each other with

kindness, empathy, and mutual respect. The emphasis on compassion shapes the perception of love as a nurturing and supportive force.

2. Mutual Rights and Responsibilities: Islamic teachings highlight the mutual rights and responsibilities of spouses. This balanced approach fosters a sense of partnership and equality, where both partners contribute to the well-being of the relationship. The emphasis on mutual respect and support enhances the perception of love as a cooperative endeavor.

3. Spiritual Practices: Shared spiritual practices, such as praying together, reading the Quran, and observing religious rituals, can strengthen the bond between Muslim partners. These practices foster spiritual intimacy and reinforce the sense of shared faith and purpose in the relationship.

Hinduism: Love as a Path to Spiritual Enlightenment

1. Bhakti (Devotion): In Hinduism, Bhakti or devotional love is a path to spiritual enlightenment. This concept influences romantic relationships by encouraging partners to approach each other with devotion, selflessness, and a desire for spiritual growth. The principles of Bhakti can deepen emotional and spiritual connections between partners.

2. Marriage as a Sacred Union: Hindu marriage is considered a sacred union that involves both spiritual and material aspects. The rituals and vows taken during the marriage ceremony emphasize the spiritual significance of the partnership. The belief that marriage is a dharma (duty) reinforces the commitment to maintaining a harmonious and loving relationship.

3. Connection to the Divine: Hinduism teaches that love between partners can reflect the divine love between the individual soul (Atman) and the universal soul (Brahman). This perspective elevates the perception of romantic love to a spiritual practice that fosters a deeper connection to the divine.

Buddhism: Compassionate and Mindful Love

1. Loving-Kindness (Metta): In Buddhism, the practice of loving-kindness (Metta) involves cultivating unconditional love and compassion for all beings. This practice influences romantic relationships by encouraging partners to approach each other with empathy, patience, and selflessness. The emphasis on Metta fosters a compassionate and nurturing perception of love.

2. Mindfulness and Presence: Mindfulness, or being fully present in the moment, is a central tenet of Buddhism. In romantic relationships, mindfulness helps partners to truly

listen to each other, appreciate their time together, and respond to each other's needs with attentiveness and care. This mindful approach enhances emotional intimacy and connection.

3. Non-Attachment: Buddhism teaches the principle of non-attachment, which involves letting go of clinging and possessiveness. In the context of romantic relationships, non-attachment encourages partners to love each other freely and without conditions, fostering a sense of mutual respect and freedom.

Judaism: Covenant and Commitment

1. Ahava (Love) and Chesed (Loving-Kindness): In Judaism, Ahava (love) and Chesed (loving-kindness) are central to romantic relationships. These concepts emphasize enduring love, compassion, and mutual support. The principles of Ahava and Chesed shape the perception of love as a commitment to care for and uplift one's partner.

2. Marriage as a Covenant: Jewish marriage (kiddushin) is viewed as a covenantal relationship that reflects the bond between God and the Jewish people. This covenant emphasizes mutual obligations, respect, and the intention to build a family and community based on Jewish values. The covenantal perspective reinforces the commitment to maintaining a loving and supportive relationship.

3. Spiritual Practices: Jewish couples often engage in rituals and practices that reinforce their spiritual bond, such as observing Shabbat together, participating in holiday celebrations, and engaging in regular study of Torah. These shared religious activities strengthen the couple's connection to each other and their faith.

Taoism: Harmony and Balance in Love

1. Yin and Yang: The Taoist concept of Yin and Yang represents the complementary forces that create balance in the universe. In romantic relationships, this principle encourages partners to embrace their differences and seek harmony, recognizing that both masculine (Yang) and feminine (Yin) energies are essential for a balanced partnership.

2. The Way (Tao) of Love: Taoism teaches that love should flow naturally, without force or manipulation. By following the Tao, or the natural way, couples can cultivate a relationship that is harmonious, spontaneous, and aligned with the natural rhythms of life. This perspective fosters a perception of love as a harmonious and balanced force.

3. Energy and Intimacy: Taoist practices, such as Tai Chi and Qigong, focus on cultivating and balancing the body's energy (Qi). In the context of romantic love, these practices

can enhance intimacy and connection by promoting physical and emotional well-being.

Indigenous and Ancestral Beliefs: Love as Connection to the Earth and Community

1. Sacred Union and Community: In many Indigenous cultures, marriage and romantic relationships are seen as sacred unions that contribute to the well-being of the community. The health and harmony of the relationship are considered vital for the prosperity of the entire community. This communal perspective shapes the perception of love as a collective and interconnected experience.

2. Rituals and Ceremonies: Indigenous cultures often incorporate rituals and ceremonies to honor romantic unions. These ceremonies may involve the blessing of the natural elements, the guidance of ancestors, and the participation of the community, emphasizing the spiritual significance of the partnership. These practices reinforce the sacred and communal nature of love.

3. Connection to the Earth: Indigenous beliefs often highlight the importance of living in harmony with the Earth. In romantic relationships, this connection to nature can foster a deep sense of grounding, balance, and respect for the interconnectedness of all life. The perception of love as a

connection to the Earth and community enriches the spiritual dimension of the relationship.

Spirituality and faith profoundly influence how individuals perceive and experience romantic love. These elements provide a framework for understanding love as a divine and transcendent force that shapes our relationships and guides our behaviors. By exploring the spiritual dimensions of love across different religions and belief systems, we gain a deeper appreciation of love's transformative power and its role in our journey toward personal and collective growth.

As we continue our exploration in this book, we will delve into the health and psychological benefits of romantic love, examining how love impacts our well-being and mental health. Through this journey, we aim to uncover the many layers that contribute to our understanding of love, enriching our appreciation of this powerful and transformative force in human life.

CHAPTER 06

LOVE AND HEALTH

Romantic love is often celebrated for its emotional and spiritual significance, but it also has profound effects on physical and mental health. The experience of being in a loving relationship can lead to numerous health benefits, enhancing overall well-being and longevity. In this chapter, we will examine the physical and mental health benefits of experiencing romantic love, exploring how love influences our bodies and minds in positive ways.

Physical Health Benefits of Romantic Love

Romantic love can lead to various physical health benefits, contributing to improved cardiovascular health, immune function, and overall longevity. These benefits are often mediated through physiological processes and behavioral changes associated with being in a loving relationship.

1. Cardiovascular Health

Research has shown that being in a loving relationship can have a positive impact on cardiovascular health. Several factors contribute to this benefit:

- Lower Blood Pressure: Studies have found that individuals in supportive, loving relationships tend to have lower blood pressure compared to those who are single or in stressful relationships. The emotional support and companionship provided by a loving partner can help reduce stress and promote relaxation, leading to better cardiovascular health.

- Reduced Risk of Heart Disease: Married individuals or those in long-term committed relationships often have a lower risk of developing heart disease. The emotional and practical support provided by a partner can encourage healthier lifestyle choices, such as regular exercise, a balanced diet, and adherence to medical advice.

2. Enhanced Immune Function

Romantic love can also boost immune function, making individuals more resilient to illnesses and infections. The following factors contribute to this benefit:

- Reduced Stress Levels: Chronic stress can weaken the immune system, making individuals more susceptible to illnesses. Being in a loving relationship can help reduce stress levels through emotional support, physical affection, and the presence of a reliable partner.

- Positive Hormonal Changes: The hormones associated with love and affection, such as oxytocin and endorphins, can enhance immune function. Oxytocin, often referred to as the "love hormone," promotes relaxation and reduces inflammation, contributing to a stronger immune response.

3. Increased Longevity

Several studies have found that individuals in loving relationships tend to live longer than their single counterparts. This increased longevity can be attributed to several factors:

- Emotional Support: Having a loving partner provides a source of emotional support, which can help individuals cope with life's challenges and reduce the risk of mental health issues, such as depression and anxiety.

- Healthier Lifestyle Choices: Partners often encourage each other to adopt healthier habits, such as regular physical activity, nutritious eating, and avoiding harmful behaviors like smoking or excessive drinking. These lifestyle choices contribute to better overall health and longevity.

Mental Health Benefits of Romantic Love

Romantic love has a significant impact on mental health, promoting emotional well-being, resilience, and overall life satisfaction. The presence of a loving partner can provide a sense of security, belonging, and happiness, which are crucial for mental health.

1. Emotional Support and Resilience

One of the most important mental health benefits of romantic love is the emotional support provided by a partner. This support can enhance resilience and help individuals navigate life's challenges more effectively:

- Reduced Risk of Depression: Studies have shown that individuals in loving relationships are less likely to experience depression compared to those who are single or in unhappy relationships. The emotional support and companionship of a loving partner can help buffer against the effects of stress and adversity.

- Increased Resilience: Having a supportive partner can enhance resilience, allowing individuals to cope more effectively with life's challenges. The presence of a loving partner provides a source of strength and encouragement, helping individuals to persevere through difficult times.

2. Improved Self-Esteem and Self-Worth

Being in a loving relationship can positively impact self-esteem and self-worth. The validation and affirmation provided by a partner can enhance an individual's sense of value and self-confidence:

- Positive Reinforcement: A loving partner often provides positive reinforcement and validation, which can boost self-esteem. This affirmation helps individuals feel valued and appreciated, contributing to a healthier self-image.

- Reduced Feelings of Loneliness: Romantic love can reduce feelings of loneliness and isolation, which are often associated with low self-esteem and mental health issues. The companionship and emotional connection provided by a loving partner can foster a sense of belonging and community.

3. Enhanced Emotional Well-Being

Romantic love contributes to overall emotional well-being by promoting happiness, contentment, and emotional stability. The following factors contribute to this benefit:

- Oxytocin and Emotional Bonding: Oxytocin, the hormone associated with love and bonding, plays a crucial role in emotional well-being. The release of oxytocin during physical affection and emotional connection can promote feelings of happiness, calm, and emotional security.

- Reduced Anxiety and Stress: The presence of a loving partner can help reduce anxiety and stress levels. Knowing that there is someone who cares and supports you can provide a sense of security and stability, which is essential for emotional well-being.

The Role of Intimacy in Health

Intimacy, both emotional and physical, plays a vital role in the health benefits associated with romantic love. The close connection and affection shared between partners can enhance both physical and mental health:

1. Physical Intimacy and Health

Physical intimacy, such as hugging, kissing, and sexual activity, has numerous health benefits:

- Release of Endorphins: Physical intimacy triggers the release of endorphins, which are natural painkillers and mood enhancers. This release can reduce pain, alleviate stress, and promote a sense of well-being.

- Improved Sleep: Sexual activity can promote better sleep quality by releasing oxytocin and reducing stress levels. Adequate sleep is crucial for overall health and well-being.

2. Emotional Intimacy and Connection

Emotional intimacy, characterized by open communication, trust, and mutual understanding, enhances mental health:

- Building Trust and Security: Emotional intimacy fosters a sense of trust and security in the relationship, which is essential for mental health. Knowing that you can rely on your partner provides emotional stability and reduces anxiety.

- Promoting Open Communication: Open and honest communication is a key aspect of emotional intimacy. Being able to express feelings, concerns, and desires without fear of judgment promotes emotional well-being and strengthens the relationship.

Challenges and Considerations

While romantic love has numerous health benefits, it is important to recognize that not all relationships are beneficial. Unhealthy relationships characterized by conflict, stress, and lack of support can have negative effects on both physical and mental health:

1. The Impact of Unhealthy Relationships

- Stress and Anxiety: Relationships characterized by constant conflict and stress can contribute to increased levels of anxiety and chronic stress, negatively impacting health.

- Mental Health Issues: Unhealthy relationships can exacerbate mental health issues such as depression, low self-esteem, and emotional instability.

2. The Importance of Healthy Relationship Dynamics

- Communication and Support: Healthy relationships are built on effective communication, mutual support, and respect. These dynamics are crucial for reaping the health benefits associated with romantic love.

- Seeking Help: For individuals in unhealthy relationships, seeking help from therapists, counselors, or support groups can be essential for improving relationship dynamics and overall well-being.

Romantic love has profound effects on both physical and mental health. From improved cardiovascular health and enhanced immune function to emotional resilience and increased self-esteem, the benefits of being in a loving relationship are extensive. However, it is important to cultivate healthy relationship dynamics characterized by communication, support, and mutual respect to fully experience these benefits.

As we continue our exploration in this book, we will delve into the ways romantic love contributes to personal growth and fulfillment, examining how love can be a catalyst for self-discovery and life satisfaction. Through this journey, we aim to uncover the many layers that contribute to our understanding of love, enriching our appreciation of this powerful and transformative force in human life.

Love and Health

Romantic love is often celebrated for its emotional and spiritual significance, but it also has profound effects on physical and mental health. The experience of being in a loving relationship can lead to numerous health benefits, enhancing overall well-being and longevity. In this chapter, we will examine how love impacts well-being, stress levels, and overall life satisfaction. By understanding these effects, we can appreciate the transformative power of romantic love on our health and happiness.

Impact of Love on Well-Being

Romantic love significantly enhances overall well-being, contributing to a sense of happiness, fulfillment, and emotional stability. The positive effects of love on well-being can be attributed to several key factors:

1. Emotional Support and Security

One of the primary benefits of being in a loving relationship is the emotional support and security it provides. Having a partner who offers understanding, empathy, and encouragement can greatly enhance emotional well-being.

- Sense of Belonging: Romantic love fosters a sense of belonging and connection, which is crucial for emotional health. Knowing that there is someone who cares deeply for you and is committed to your well-being can create a profound sense of security and comfort.

- Emotional Safety: A loving relationship provides a safe space to express emotions, share vulnerabilities, and seek comfort during difficult times. This emotional safety promotes mental health and resilience.

2. Increased Happiness and Life Satisfaction

Love is strongly associated with increased happiness and overall life satisfaction. Being in a loving relationship can bring joy, contentment, and a sense of purpose.

- Positive Emotions: Romantic love often generates positive emotions such as joy, excitement, and gratitude. These emotions contribute to overall happiness and life satisfaction.

- Life Purpose and Meaning: Being in a committed relationship can give individuals a sense of purpose and direction. Shared goals, mutual support, and the desire to build a future together can provide meaning and fulfillment.

3. Enhanced Self-Esteem and Confidence

Romantic love can have a positive impact on self-esteem and confidence. The validation and affirmation received from a loving partner can enhance an individual's sense of self-worth.

- Affirmation and Validation: A loving partner often provides positive reinforcement, compliments, and encouragement, which can boost self-esteem. Feeling valued and appreciated by someone you love can enhance self-confidence.

- Reduced Feelings of Loneliness: Romantic love can reduce feelings of loneliness and isolation, which are often linked to low self-esteem and mental health issues. The companionship and emotional connection provided by a loving partner foster a sense of belonging and self-worth.

Impact of Love on Stress Levels

Romantic love plays a crucial role in managing and reducing stress levels. The presence of a supportive partner can buffer against the negative effects of stress and promote relaxation and well-being.

1. Emotional Support and Stress Reduction

Having a loving partner who provides emotional support can significantly reduce stress levels. The ability to share concerns, seek comfort, and receive encouragement can alleviate stress and promote emotional resilience.

- Stress Buffering: The support provided by a loving partner can act as a buffer against the negative effects of stress. Knowing that there is someone who cares and supports you can mitigate the impact of stressors and promote a sense of calm and security.

- Emotional Comfort: Physical affection, such as hugging, kissing, and cuddling, can release oxytocin, a hormone associated with relaxation and stress reduction. This physical connection promotes emotional comfort and reduces stress levels.

2. Improved Coping Mechanisms

Being in a loving relationship can improve coping mechanisms and resilience. The presence of a supportive partner can enhance an individual's ability to manage stress and navigate challenges.

- Collaborative Problem-Solving: Loving partners often work together to address challenges and find solutions. This collaborative approach can reduce stress by providing practical support and shared responsibility.

- Enhanced Resilience: The emotional strength gained from being in a loving relationship can enhance resilience. The sense of security and support provided by a loving partner can help individuals cope more effectively with stress and adversity.

3. Positive Lifestyle Changes

Romantic love can encourage positive lifestyle changes that reduce stress and promote overall well-being. Partners often influence each other's habits and behaviors in beneficial ways.

- Healthy Habits: Loving partners often encourage each other to adopt healthy habits, such as regular exercise, a balanced diet, and adequate sleep. These healthy habits can reduce stress and improve overall well-being.

- Mutual Support: Partners can support each other in managing stress through relaxation techniques, such as mindfulness, meditation, and deep breathing exercises. Engaging in these practices together can enhance relaxation and reduce stress levels.

Impact of Love on Overall Life Satisfaction

Romantic love contributes significantly to overall life satisfaction, enhancing the quality of life and promoting a sense of fulfillment and happiness.

1. Emotional Fulfillment

Being in a loving relationship can provide deep emotional fulfillment, contributing to overall life satisfaction. The emotional connection and intimacy shared with a partner can enhance happiness and contentment.

- Deep Connection: The emotional bond shared with a loving partner provides a sense of deep connection and intimacy. This connection enhances overall life satisfaction by fulfilling emotional needs and desires.

- Shared Experiences: Sharing life experiences, joys, and challenges with a loving partner can enhance life satisfaction. The ability to create and cherish memories together contributes to a sense of fulfillment and happiness.

2. Personal Growth and Development

Romantic love can foster personal growth and development, contributing to overall life satisfaction. The support and encouragement provided by a loving partner can inspire individuals to pursue their goals and aspirations.

- Mutual Encouragement: Loving partners often encourage each other to pursue personal goals and aspirations. This mutual support fosters personal growth and development, enhancing overall life satisfaction.

- Increased Confidence: The validation and affirmation received from a loving partner can boost confidence and self-esteem. This increased confidence can inspire individuals to take on new challenges and achieve their goals, contributing to life satisfaction.

3. Sense of Purpose and Meaning

Being in a loving relationship can provide a sense of purpose and meaning, enhancing overall life satisfaction. The commitment and shared goals of a loving partnership contribute to a fulfilling and meaningful life.

- Shared Goals: Loving partners often have shared goals and aspirations, such as building a family, creating a home, or pursuing common interests. These shared goals provide a sense of purpose and direction, enhancing life satisfaction.

- Life Meaning: The experience of loving and being loved can give life profound meaning. The emotional connection and commitment shared with a partner contribute to a fulfilling and meaningful life.

Romantic love has a profound impact on well-being, stress levels, and overall life satisfaction. The emotional support, companionship, and intimacy provided by a loving partner contribute to improved emotional and physical health, reduced stress, and a greater sense of fulfillment and happiness. By understanding the transformative power of love, we can appreciate its vital role in enhancing our health and overall quality of life.

As we continue our exploration in this book, we will delve into the ways romantic love contributes to personal growth and fulfillment, examining how love can be a catalyst for self-discovery and life satisfaction. Through this journey, we aim to uncover the many layers that contribute to our understanding of love, enriching our appreciation of this powerful and transformative force in human life.

97

CHAPTER 07

THE SOURCE OF LOVE

Love is a profound and complex emotion that has intrigued philosophers, theologians, and thinkers for centuries. Understanding the origin of love involves exploring its philosophical and theological dimensions. In this chapter, we will delve into various perspectives on the source of love, examining how different traditions and schools of thought have interpreted its origins. By exploring these perspectives, we can gain a deeper appreciation of love as a fundamental aspect of human existence.

Philosophical Perspectives on the Origin of Love

Philosophy offers a rich tapestry of ideas and theories about the nature and origin of love. Philosophers have pondered the essence of love, its purpose, and its role in human life, providing diverse insights into its source.

1. Plato's Concept of Love

Plato, one of the most influential philosophers in Western thought, offered profound insights into the nature of love in his work "The Symposium." According to Plato, love (or Eros) is a powerful force that drives individuals toward the pursuit of beauty and truth.

- The Ladder of Love: Plato describes a metaphorical "ladder of love," where individuals begin by appreciating physical beauty and gradually ascend to higher forms of love, culminating in the love of the Form of Beauty itself. This ascent represents the soul's journey towards divine understanding and enlightenment.

- Love as a Motivating Force: For Plato, love is a motivating force that inspires individuals to seek higher truths and achieve personal growth. It is a desire for the eternal and the perfect, transcending physical attraction and leading to spiritual fulfillment.

2. Aristotle's View on Love

Aristotle, a student of Plato, offered a more practical and grounded perspective on love. In his work "Nicomachean Ethics," Aristotle discusses love as a virtue and a key component of friendship.

- Types of Love: Aristotle distinguishes between different types of love, including philia (friendship), eros (romantic love), and agape (selfless love). He emphasizes the importance of philia, or virtuous friendship, which is based on mutual respect, shared values, and the pursuit of the good life.

- Love and Virtue: For Aristotle, love is closely linked to virtue. True love involves a commitment to the well-being of the other person and the cultivation of virtuous qualities such as kindness, generosity, and integrity. Love, in this sense, is both a moral and an emotional bond.

3. Existentialist Perspectives on Love

Existentialist philosophers, such as Jean-Paul Sartre and Simone de Beauvoir, explore love in the context of human freedom, individuality, and existential choice.

- Freedom and Love: Sartre argues that love involves a delicate balance between freedom and commitment. While love requires a deep connection and commitment to another person, it must also respect the freedom and autonomy of both partners. Sartre emphasizes the importance of authentic love, which acknowledges and embraces the inherent freedom of each individual.

- Love as an Act of Creation: Simone de Beauvoir views love as an act of creation and mutual recognition. She suggests that love involves recognizing and affirming the unique subjectivity of the other person, creating a shared reality where both partners can grow and thrive. Love, for de Beauvoir, is a dynamic and evolving relationship that requires continuous effort and engagement.

Theological Perspectives on the Origin of Love

Theology offers profound insights into the divine and spiritual dimensions of love. Various religious traditions provide unique perspectives on the origin and nature of love, often viewing it as a reflection of divine love or a fundamental aspect of the divine nature.

1. Christianity: Love as Divine Nature

In Christianity, love is seen as a fundamental aspect of God's nature and a reflection of divine love for humanity. The Christian understanding of love is deeply rooted in the teachings of Jesus and the writings of the New Testament.

- Agape Love: The concept of agape, or selfless, unconditional love, is central to Christian theology. Agape love is exemplified by God's love for humanity, as demonstrated through the life and sacrifice of Jesus Christ. Christians are called to emulate this divine love in their relationships with others.

- The Greatest Commandment: Jesus teaches that the greatest commandment is to love God with all one's heart, soul, and mind, and to love one's neighbor as oneself (Matthew 22:37-39). This emphasis on love as the highest moral principle underscores its divine origin and significance in the Christian faith.

2. Islam: Love as a Reflection of Divine Compassion

In Islam, love is viewed as a reflection of divine compassion and mercy. The Quran and Hadith provide guidance on the importance of love in human relationships and the relationship between humans and God.

- Rahmah and Mawaddah: The Quran uses the terms "rahmah" (mercy) and "mawaddah" (affection) to describe the ideal qualities of love in marriage and relationships. These principles emphasize the importance of compassion, kindness, and mutual support as reflections of God's love for humanity.

- Divine Love and Devotion: Islamic mysticism, or Sufism, places a strong emphasis on divine love and devotion. Sufi poets and mystics, such as Rumi, explore the theme of divine love as a path to spiritual enlightenment and union with God. Love, in this context, is both a human and a divine experience.

3. Hinduism: Love as a Path to Moksha

In Hinduism, love is seen as a powerful force that can lead to spiritual growth and liberation (moksha). The various forms of love described in Hindu texts highlight its spiritual dimensions and transformative potential.

- Bhakti (Devotional Love): Bhakti, or devotional love, is a central concept in Hinduism. It involves a deep, selfless devotion to a deity, which can lead to spiritual enlightenment and union with the divine. The principles of Bhakti can also be applied to human relationships, encouraging selflessness and compassion.

- The Kama Sutra: The Kama Sutra, an ancient Hindu text, explores the art of love and relationships. While often misunderstood as purely a manual on sexual positions, the Kama Sutra also delves into the emotional and spiritual aspects of love, offering guidance on cultivating deep, meaningful connections.

4. Buddhism: Compassionate and Mindful Love

In Buddhism, love is understood through the principles of compassion (karuna) and loving-kindness (metta). These principles provide a framework for understanding love as a path to spiritual growth and enlightenment.

- Metta (Loving-Kindness): Metta involves cultivating unconditional love and compassion for all beings. In romantic relationships, practicing Metta encourages partners to approach each other with empathy, patience, and selflessness, fostering a compassionate and nurturing connection.

- Non-Attachment: Buddhism teaches the principle of non-attachment, which involves letting go of clinging and possessiveness. In the context of love, non-attachment encourages partners to love each other freely and without conditions, promoting a sense of mutual respect and freedom.

Indigenous and Ancestral Beliefs: Love as Connection to the Earth and Community

Many Indigenous and ancestral belief systems emphasize the interconnectedness of all life and the importance of community and relationship with the natural world. These principles deeply influence their understanding of the origin and nature of love.

1. Sacred Union and Community

In many Indigenous cultures, marriage and romantic relationships are seen as sacred unions that contribute to the well-being of the community. The health and harmony of the relationship are considered vital for the prosperity of the entire community.

- Rituals and Ceremonies: Indigenous cultures often incorporate rituals and ceremonies to honor romantic unions. These ceremonies may involve the blessing of the natural elements, the guidance of ancestors, and the participation of the community, emphasizing the spiritual significance of the partnership.

2. Connection to the Earth

Indigenous beliefs often highlight the importance of living in harmony with the Earth. In romantic relationships, this connection to nature can foster a deep sense of grounding, balance, and respect for the interconnectedness of all life.

- Love as Interconnectedness: The perception of love as a connection to the Earth and community enriches the spiritual dimension of the relationship. This perspective emphasizes the interconnectedness of all beings and the importance of maintaining harmony with the natural world.

Philosophical and theological perspectives on the origin of love offer profound insights into its nature and significance. From the philosophical explorations of Plato and Aristotle to the theological teachings of Christianity, Islam, Hinduism, Buddhism, and Indigenous beliefs, love is viewed as a divine and transformative force that shapes human relationships and guides our behaviors.

By exploring these diverse perspectives, we gain a deeper understanding of love as a fundamental aspect of human existence, transcending physical and emotional dimensions to touch the realms of the spiritual and the divine. This enriched understanding of the source of love enhances our appreciation of its power and significance in our lives.

As we continue our exploration in this book, we will delve into how love contributes to personal growth and fulfillment, examining how love can be a catalyst for self-discovery and life satisfaction. Through this journey, we aim to uncover the many layers that contribute to our understanding of love, enriching our appreciation of this powerful and transformative force in human life.

The Source of Love

The concept of divine love is a cornerstone of many religious and spiritual traditions. It represents the highest form of love, characterized by selflessness, unconditionality, and an all-encompassing nature. Understanding divine love provides profound insights into human relationships, offering a model for how we can love one another more deeply and authentically. In this chapter, we will explore the concept of divine love and its implications for human relationships, examining how this transcendent form of love can transform and elevate our connections with others.

Divine Love in Various Religious Traditions

Different religious traditions offer unique perspectives on divine love, each contributing to a richer understanding of its nature and implications.

1. Christianity: Agape Love

In Christianity, agape is the term used to describe the selfless, unconditional love of God for humanity and the love that humans are called to share with one another.

- God's Love for Humanity: The Christian concept of agape love is epitomized by God's love for humanity, which is unconditional, sacrificial, and everlasting. This love is most clearly demonstrated in the life and sacrifice of Jesus Christ, who, according to Christian belief, died for the sins of humanity to offer salvation and eternal life.

- Implications for Human Relationships: Christians are called to emulate this divine love in their relationships. Agape love in human relationships involves selflessness, forgiveness, and a commitment to the well-being of others. It encourages individuals to love others without expecting anything in return, reflecting the boundless and unconditional nature of divine love.

2. Islam: Rahmah and Divine Compassion

In Islam, divine love is often expressed through the concepts of rahmah (mercy) and compassion, which are central attributes of Allah.

- Divine Compassion: Allah's love for humanity is described as compassionate and merciful, with countless references in the Quran to God's kindness and forgiveness.

This divine compassion is seen as a model for how Muslims should treat others.

- Implications for Human Relationships: The emphasis on rahmah in human relationships encourages Muslims to act with kindness, empathy, and forgiveness. These qualities are seen as reflections of divine love and are essential for building harmonious and supportive relationships.

3. Hinduism: Bhakti and Devotional Love

In Hinduism, the concept of bhakti represents devotional love towards a deity, characterized by intense devotion and personal attachment.

- Devotion to the Divine: Bhakti involves a deep, personal relationship with the divine, where the devotee offers love and service to a deity with complete selflessness and surrender. This form of love is seen as a path to spiritual liberation and union with the divine.

- Implications for Human Relationships: Bhakti teaches that true love involves selflessness, dedication, and the desire to uplift and support others. This principle can be applied to human relationships, encouraging individuals to love their partners and others with the same devotion and selflessness that they offer to the divine.

4. Buddhism: Metta and Loving-Kindness

In Buddhism, the concept of metta, or loving-kindness, represents an unconditional and universal love that extends to all beings.

- Loving-Kindness: Metta is a practice of cultivating unconditional love and compassion for all beings, without discrimination or attachment. It involves wishing others well and acting in ways that promote their happiness and well-being.

- Implications for Human Relationships: Practicing metta in human relationships involves approaching others with kindness, empathy, and a genuine desire for their happiness. It encourages individuals to cultivate a loving and compassionate attitude towards all beings, fostering harmonious and supportive relationships.

Implications of Divine Love for Human Relationships

Understanding and embracing the concept of divine love can have transformative effects on human relationships. It offers a model for how we can love one another more deeply and authentically, with implications for various aspects of our connections with others.

1. Selflessness and Altruism

Divine love is inherently selfless, characterized by a genuine concern for the well-being of others without expecting anything in return.

- Altruistic Love: Embracing the selflessness of divine love encourages individuals to act with altruism in their relationships. This means putting the needs and happiness of others before one's own and offering love and support without conditions or expectations.

- Sacrificial Love: Divine love often involves sacrifice, as seen in many religious narratives. In human relationships, this translates to making sacrifices for the well-being and happiness of others, whether it's through time, effort, or resources.

2. Unconditional Acceptance

Divine love is unconditional, offering acceptance and love regardless of one's actions or circumstances.

- Unconditional Love: Applying this principle to human relationships means loving others without conditions or prerequisites. It involves accepting others as they are, with all their flaws and imperfections, and offering love and support without judgment or criticism.

- Forgiveness: Unconditional love also involves forgiveness, recognizing that everyone makes mistakes and that holding onto resentment only harms the relationship. Embracing divine love means practicing forgiveness and moving forward with compassion and understanding.

3. Compassion and Empathy

Divine love is deeply compassionate, characterized by a profound empathy and understanding of the suffering and needs of others.

- Empathetic Love: Cultivating divine love in human relationships involves developing empathy and understanding for others. This means truly listening to and seeking to understand the experiences and emotions of those we love, and responding with compassion and support.

- Acts of Kindness: Compassionate love is expressed through acts of kindness and support. Whether it's offering a listening ear, providing practical help, or simply being there for someone in times of need, these acts of kindness reflect the compassion inherent in divine love.

4. Commitment and Fidelity

Divine love is often seen as unwavering and eternal, characterized by a deep commitment and fidelity.

- Committed Love: Emulating divine love in human relationships means cultivating a deep commitment to those we love. This involves staying true to our promises and being reliable and dependable partners, friends, and family members.

- Loyalty and Faithfulness: Divine love teaches us the importance of loyalty and faithfulness in relationships. Being faithful to our commitments and standing by those we love through thick and thin fosters trust and strengthens the bonds of love.

Challenges in Embracing Divine Love

While the principles of divine love offer a powerful model for human relationships, embodying these ideals can be challenging. It requires ongoing effort, self-reflection, and a willingness to grow and evolve.

1. Overcoming Self-Centeredness

One of the biggest challenges in embracing divine love is overcoming self-centeredness and the tendency to prioritize our own needs and desires over those of others.

- Practicing Selflessness: Cultivating divine love involves practicing selflessness in daily life. This means making a conscious effort to put the needs and happiness of others before our own and finding joy in giving and supporting those we love.

2. Letting Go of Judgment

Embracing divine love requires letting go of judgment and accepting others as they are.

- Non-Judgmental Love: Practicing non-judgmental love involves recognizing that everyone has flaws and imperfections and that these do not diminish their worthiness of love and compassion. It means offering love and support without conditions or criticism.

3. Cultivating Compassion and Empathy

Developing true compassion and empathy requires ongoing effort and self-reflection.

- Empathy Practices: Engaging in practices that cultivate empathy, such as mindfulness, active listening, and putting oneself in others' shoes, can help deepen our understanding and compassion for those we love.

The concept of divine love offers profound insights into how we can love one another more deeply and authentically. By understanding and embracing the principles of selflessness, unconditional acceptance, compassion, and commitment inherent in divine love, we can transform our human relationships and create deeper, more meaningful connections.

As we continue our exploration in this book, we will delve into how romantic love contributes to personal growth and fulfillment, examining how love can be a catalyst for self-discovery and life satisfaction. Through this journey, we aim to uncover the many layers that contribute to our understanding of love, enriching our appreciation of this powerful and transformative force in human life.

CHAPTER 08

LOVE AND PROSPERITY

The connection between love and prosperity is profound and multifaceted. Love, in its various forms, can significantly influence an individual's sense of well-being, drive for success, and overall prosperity. In this chapter, we will investigate the relationship between love, prosperity, and success in life. By examining how love fosters personal and professional growth, supports emotional and financial stability, and enhances overall life satisfaction, we can better understand the transformative power of love in achieving prosperity.

The Impact of Love on Personal Growth and Success

Romantic love, familial love, and the love of friends all contribute to personal growth and success in various ways.

The emotional support and encouragement provided by loving relationships can inspire individuals to pursue their goals and achieve their full potential.

1. Emotional Support and Confidence

One of the most significant ways love contributes to personal growth is through the emotional support it provides. Having a loving partner, supportive family, or close friends can bolster an individual's confidence and self-esteem.

- Encouragement and Motivation: Loving relationships often provide encouragement and motivation to pursue personal and professional goals. The belief and support of loved ones can inspire individuals to take risks and strive for success.

- Resilience and Coping: Love also enhances resilience, helping individuals cope with setbacks and challenges. The presence of a supportive partner or network can provide the strength and reassurance needed to overcome obstacles and persist in the face of adversity.

2. Enhanced Communication and Interpersonal Skills

Love fosters the development of communication and interpersonal skills, which are crucial for success in both personal and professional settings.

- Effective Communication: Loving relationships require effective communication, including active listening, empathy, and clear expression of thoughts and feelings. These skills are transferable to professional environments, enhancing teamwork, leadership, and conflict resolution.

- Building Trust and Collaboration: Love teaches the importance of trust and collaboration. In the workplace, these principles can lead to more effective teamwork, stronger professional relationships, and a more harmonious work environment.

3. Inspiration and Creativity

Love can be a powerful source of inspiration and creativity, driving individuals to explore new ideas and achieve excellence in their endeavors.

- Creative Expression: Romantic love and deep emotional connections often inspire creative expression in art, music, writing, and other forms of creative work. The emotions and experiences associated with love can fuel artistic and innovative endeavors.

- Innovation and Problem-Solving: The support and encouragement of loved ones can also foster a mindset of innovation and creative problem-solving. Feeling secure and valued in a loving relationship can give individuals the confidence to think outside the box and pursue novel solutions.

The Role of Love in Financial Prosperity

Love plays a crucial role in financial prosperity by influencing financial behaviors, decision-making, and overall financial stability. Loving relationships can provide the support and partnership needed to achieve financial goals and build wealth.

1. Shared Financial Goals and Planning

In romantic relationships, love fosters the development of shared financial goals and collaborative financial planning.

- Joint Financial Planning: Couples who love and trust each other are more likely to engage in joint financial planning, setting shared goals for saving, investing, and spending. This collaborative approach can lead to more effective financial management and long-term financial stability.

- Mutual Support: Loving partners often support each other's financial goals and aspirations, whether it's pursuing further education, starting a business, or investing in a new venture. This mutual support can enhance financial success and prosperity.

2. Financial Stability and Security

Loving relationships contribute to financial stability and security, providing a safety net during times of financial uncertainty or crisis.

- Dual Incomes: In dual-income households, the combined earnings of both partners can lead to greater financial stability and the ability to build wealth more effectively. Shared financial responsibilities can reduce the financial burden on each individual.

- Support During Hard Times: Loving relationships provide emotional and practical support during financial hardships. Having a supportive partner or family can help individuals navigate financial challenges and make more informed and rational decisions.

3. Healthy Financial Behaviors

Love can influence healthy financial behaviors, promoting responsible spending, saving, and investing habits.

- Responsible Spending: Loving partners often influence each other's spending behaviors, encouraging responsible and mindful spending. This can lead to better financial management and the avoidance of unnecessary debt.

- Saving and Investing: Couples in loving relationships are more likely to prioritize saving and investing for the future. The desire to build a secure and prosperous future together can motivate individuals to adopt prudent financial practices.

Love and Overall Life Satisfaction

The relationship between love and overall life satisfaction is well-documented. Loving relationships significantly enhance emotional well-being and contribute to a fulfilling and prosperous life.

1. Happiness and Well-Being

Love is a key contributor to happiness and emotional well-being, which are essential components of overall life satisfaction.

- Emotional Fulfillment: Loving relationships provide emotional fulfillment, creating a sense of joy, contentment, and purpose. The deep emotional connection and intimacy shared with loved ones enhance overall happiness.

- Reduced Stress and Anxiety: The emotional support provided by loving relationships can reduce stress and anxiety, promoting mental health and well-being. Knowing that there is someone who cares deeply for you provides a sense of security and comfort.

2. Sense of Purpose and Meaning

Love gives life a sense of purpose and meaning, enriching the overall experience of living.

- Shared Goals and Aspirations: Loving relationships often involve shared goals and aspirations, whether it's building a family, creating a home, or pursuing common interests. These shared endeavors provide a sense of purpose and direction.

- Legacy and Impact: Love inspires individuals to leave a positive legacy and make a meaningful impact on the lives of others. The desire to support and uplift loved ones can drive individuals to contribute positively to their communities and the world.

3. Quality of Life

Loving relationships enhance the overall quality of life by fostering emotional, social, and physical well-being.

- Social Connection: Love fosters social connections and a sense of belonging, which are crucial for overall life satisfaction. Strong social networks and loving relationships provide a support system that enhances quality of life.

- Health Benefits: The health benefits of love, including improved cardiovascular health, enhanced immune function, and increased longevity, contribute to a higher quality of life. Loving relationships promote healthy behaviors and provide emotional support that enhances physical health.

Challenges and Considerations

While love has the potential to significantly enhance prosperity and success, it is important to recognize and address the challenges that can arise in loving relationships.

1. Balancing Love and Ambition

Balancing the demands of a loving relationship with personal and professional ambitions can be challenging.

- Communication and Compromise: Effective communication and compromise are essential for balancing love and ambition. Partners need to openly discuss their goals and find ways to support each other's aspirations while maintaining a strong and loving relationship.

- Setting Boundaries: Setting healthy boundaries is important for maintaining a balance between personal and professional life. Partners should respect each other's need for time and space to pursue their individual goals.

2. Managing Financial Differences

Financial differences and disagreements can strain loving relationships.

- Open Communication: Open and honest communication about financial matters is crucial for managing financial differences. Partners should discuss their financial goals, values, and habits to find common ground and create a shared financial plan.

- Seeking Professional Advice: In some cases, seeking professional financial advice can help partners navigate complex financial issues and develop a comprehensive financial strategy that supports their goals and enhances their financial stability.

3. Maintaining Emotional Health

Maintaining emotional health and well-being is essential for fostering loving and supportive relationships.

- Self-Care: Practicing self-care and prioritizing mental health are important for maintaining emotional well-being. Partners should support each other's self-care routines and encourage healthy habits.

- Seeking Support: Seeking support from therapists, counselors, or support groups can be beneficial for addressing emotional challenges and strengthening the relationship. Professional support can provide valuable tools and strategies for maintaining a healthy and loving partnership.

The relationship between love, prosperity, and success is profound and multifaceted. Love fosters personal growth, enhances financial stability, and contributes to overall life satisfaction. By understanding and embracing the transformative power of love, we can create deeper, more meaningful relationships and achieve greater prosperity and success in life.

As we continue our exploration in this book, we will delve into how romantic love contributes to personal growth and fulfillment, examining how love can be a catalyst for self-discovery and life satisfaction. Through this journey, we aim to uncover the many layers that contribute to our understanding of love, enriching our appreciation of this powerful and transformative force in human life.

Love and Prosperity

Love is a powerful force that extends beyond personal relationships, influencing personal fulfillment and societal well-being. Cultivating love—whether romantic, familial, or platonic—can lead to profound personal growth and contribute to a healthier, more compassionate society. In this chapter, we will explore how love fosters personal fulfillment and societal well-being, highlighting the transformative power of love in creating a more harmonious and prosperous world.

Cultivating Love for Personal Fulfillment

Cultivating love in its various forms can significantly enhance personal fulfillment, leading to a richer, more meaningful life. This section examines how love contributes to self-discovery, emotional well-being, and the pursuit of personal goals.

1. Self-Discovery and Personal Growth

Love plays a crucial role in self-discovery and personal growth. Being in loving relationships encourages introspection and helps individuals understand their true selves.

- Reflecting on Values and Beliefs: Loving relationships often prompt individuals to reflect on their values, beliefs, and life goals. Through deep conversations and shared experiences, partners can help each other explore their identities and aspirations.

- Encouraging Growth: Love encourages personal growth by providing a supportive environment where individuals feel safe to take risks and pursue their dreams. The encouragement and affirmation from a loving partner or friend can inspire individuals to reach their full potential.

2. Emotional Well-Being and Resilience

Emotional well-being is closely tied to the experience of love. Loving relationships provide emotional support, stability, and resilience.

- Support Systems: A strong support system, comprising loving family members and friends, is essential for emotional well-being. Knowing that there are people who care deeply about you provides a sense of security and belonging.

- Coping with Challenges: Love enhances resilience by helping individuals cope with life's challenges. The emotional support and understanding offered by loved ones can mitigate the impact of stress and adversity, promoting mental health and stability.

3. Achieving Personal Goals

Love can be a powerful motivator in achieving personal goals. The encouragement and support from loved ones can drive individuals to pursue their ambitions with greater determination and confidence.

- Motivation and Encouragement: The belief and encouragement from loved ones can motivate individuals to strive for success. Knowing that someone has faith in your abilities can boost self-confidence and determination.

- Shared Success: Achieving personal goals can be even more fulfilling when shared with loved ones. Celebrating successes and milestones with those who matter most enhances the sense of accomplishment and joy.

Cultivating Love for Societal Well-Being

The cultivation of love has far-reaching implications for societal well-being. Love fosters social cohesion, compassion, and a sense of community, contributing to a healthier and more harmonious society.

1. Social Cohesion and Community Building

Love fosters social cohesion by strengthening the bonds between individuals and communities. Loving relationships create a sense of unity and collective responsibility.

-      Building   Stronger   Communities: Loving relationships contribute to the formation of strong, interconnected communities. When individuals feel loved and supported, they are more likely to engage in community-building activities and contribute positively to society.

- Promoting Social Responsibility: Love encourages a sense of social responsibility. Individuals who experience love and compassion are more likely to extend these feelings to others, promoting social justice and collective well-being.

2. Compassion and Empathy

Cultivating love fosters compassion and empathy, essential qualities for a just and equitable society.

- Empathetic Societies: A society that values love and compassion is more likely to be empathetic and supportive. Empathy allows individuals to understand and share the feelings of others, leading to more compassionate and inclusive social policies.

- Reducing Conflict: Love and empathy can reduce social conflict by promoting understanding and cooperation. When individuals approach conflicts with empathy and a willingness to understand different perspectives, it fosters peaceful resolutions and social harmony.

3. Mental and Physical Health

The widespread cultivation of love can have significant benefits for public health, both mental and physical.

- Mental Health: Love and supportive relationships are crucial for mental health. Societies that prioritize loving relationships and emotional well-being experience lower rates of mental health issues such as depression, anxiety, and loneliness.

- Physical Health: The health benefits of love extend to physical well-being. Strong social connections and loving relationships are associated with better health outcomes, including reduced risk of chronic diseases and increased longevity.

4. Economic Prosperity

Love and social cohesion can also contribute to economic prosperity by fostering a supportive environment for economic activities.

- Collaborative Economies: Societies that value love and collaboration are more likely to have cooperative economic systems. These systems encourage mutual support, shared resources, and collective growth, leading to economic stability and prosperity.

- Workplace Well-Being: Cultivating love and compassion in the workplace can enhance employee well-being and productivity. Supportive work environments that prioritize emotional health and positive relationships lead to higher job satisfaction and better performance.

Practical Ways to Cultivate Love

Cultivating love requires intentional effort and practices that foster loving relationships and compassionate communities. Here are some practical ways to cultivate love in personal and societal contexts:

1. Practicing Gratitude

Gratitude is a powerful way to cultivate love and appreciation in relationships.

- Expressing Thanks: Regularly expressing gratitude to loved ones strengthens relationships and fosters a positive, loving environment. Simple acts of appreciation can make a significant impact on emotional well-being and connection.

- Gratitude Journals: Keeping a gratitude journal can help individuals focus on the positive aspects of their relationships and lives, promoting a loving and appreciative mindset.

2. Active Listening and Empathy

Active listening and empathy are essential for cultivating deep, meaningful connections.

- Listening with Intention: Active listening involves fully focusing on and understanding the speaker without interrupting or judging. This practice fosters empathy and strengthens emotional bonds.

- Empathy Exercises: Engaging in empathy exercises, such as putting oneself in another's shoes, can enhance understanding and compassion in relationships.

3. Acts of Kindness

Regular acts of kindness, both big and small, can cultivate a loving and compassionate environment.

- Random Acts of Kindness: Performing random acts of kindness, such as helping a neighbor or offering a compliment, fosters a sense of community and collective well-being.

- Volunteering: Volunteering for community service or charitable organizations promotes social responsibility and compassion, contributing to societal well-being.

4. Mindfulness and Presence

Practicing mindfulness and being present in relationships can deepen emotional connections and foster love.

- Mindful Communication: Mindful communication involves being fully present and attentive during interactions with loved ones. This practice enhances understanding and emotional connection.

- Meditation and Reflection: Regular meditation and reflection on love and compassion can foster a loving mindset and promote emotional well-being.

Cultivating love has profound implications for personal fulfillment and societal well-being. Love fosters personal growth, enhances emotional and physical health, and contributes to a more compassionate and harmonious society. By intentionally cultivating love in our relationships and communities, we can create a more prosperous and fulfilling world for ourselves and future generations.

As we continue our exploration in this book, we will delve into the ways romantic love contributes to personal growth and fulfillment, examining how love can be a catalyst for self-discovery and life satisfaction. Through this journey, we aim to uncover the many layers that contribute to our understanding of love, enriching our appreciation of this powerful and transformative force in human life.

CHAPTER 09

LOVE AND PURPOSE

Love is often described as one of the most profound sources of meaning and purpose in human life. Whether it is the love between partners, the bond between parents and children, or the connection among friends and community, love shapes our experiences and gives our lives direction and significance. In this chapter, we will explore how love gives meaning and purpose to life, examining the ways in which love influences our goals, values, and sense of fulfillment.

The Role of Love in Defining Life's Purpose

Love plays a critical role in defining life's purpose, guiding our actions, and shaping our aspirations. It provides a framework within which we can understand our place in the world and our relationships with others.

1. Love as a Motivator for Personal Goals

Love often acts as a powerful motivator, driving individuals to pursue personal goals and aspirations.

- Inspiration and Drive: The love and support of a partner, family, or close friends can inspire individuals to achieve their full potential. Knowing that others believe in and support us can provide the drive and determination needed to pursue ambitious goals.

- Shared Dreams: In many relationships, partners or family members share dreams and aspirations. Working towards common goals can give life a sense of purpose and direction, fostering a deeper connection and mutual support.

2. Love and Moral Values

Love significantly influences our moral values and ethical behavior. It encourages us to act with kindness, compassion, and integrity.

- Ethical Framework: Love provides an ethical framework that guides our actions and decisions. The desire to care for and protect loved ones often extends to a broader sense of social responsibility and moral behavior.

- Compassion and Empathy: Love fosters compassion and empathy, prompting us to consider the well-being of others and act in ways that promote collective good. This moral dimension of love enhances our sense of purpose by aligning our actions with our values.

Love as a Source of Fulfillment and Happiness

The experience of love is closely tied to feelings of fulfillment and happiness. Loving relationships contribute to a sense of well-being and satisfaction in life.

1. Emotional Fulfillment

Love provides deep emotional fulfillment, enhancing our overall happiness and life satisfaction.

- Sense of Belonging: Being in loving relationships creates a sense of belonging and connection. Knowing that we are valued and cared for by others fulfills a fundamental human need for social connection and emotional intimacy.

- Emotional Support: The emotional support offered by loved ones helps us navigate life's challenges and enhances our resilience. This support fosters a sense of security and contentment, contributing to overall happiness.

2. Life Satisfaction

Love plays a crucial role in achieving life satisfaction by enriching our daily experiences and providing a sense of meaning.

- Shared Joys: Sharing joys and successes with loved ones amplifies the sense of achievement and satisfaction. Celebrating milestones and accomplishments together enhances the fulfillment derived from these experiences.

- Mutual Growth: Loving relationships often involve mutual growth and development. Supporting each other's personal and professional goals creates a dynamic environment where both individuals can thrive and find satisfaction.

Love and the Search for Meaning

Love is central to the search for meaning in life. It provides a context within which we can explore our identity and purpose.

1. Identity and Self-Understanding

Love helps us understand ourselves better and shapes our identity.

- Self-Reflection: Loving relationships encourage self-reflection and personal growth. Interactions with loved ones often prompt us to examine our beliefs, values, and aspirations, leading to a deeper understanding of ourselves.

- Mirror of the Self: Loved ones act as mirrors, reflecting back our strengths and weaknesses. This reflection helps us recognize our true selves and fosters personal growth and self-improvement.

2. Life's Purpose and Direction

Love gives life purpose and direction by guiding our actions and decisions.

- Guiding Principles: The love we have for others often guides our principles and priorities. Decisions made with loved ones in mind are imbued with greater significance and purpose.

- Legacy and Impact: Love inspires us to leave a positive legacy and make a meaningful impact on the lives of others. Whether it is through raising children, contributing to our communities, or supporting causes we care about, love motivates us to create a lasting and meaningful legacy.

The Transformative Power of Love

Love has the power to transform our lives in profound ways, influencing our personal growth, relationships, and overall sense of purpose.

1. Personal Transformation

Love can lead to significant personal transformation, fostering growth and self-discovery.

- Positive Change: Loving relationships encourage positive change and self-improvement. The desire to be a better partner, parent, or friend can motivate individuals to adopt healthier habits, develop new skills, and strive for personal growth.

- Healing and Growth: Love has a healing power that can help individuals overcome past traumas and emotional wounds. The support and understanding of loved ones provide a safe space for healing and growth.

2. Transforming Relationships

Love transforms relationships, deepening connections and fostering mutual understanding and respect.

- Strengthening Bonds: Love strengthens the bonds between individuals, creating a foundation of trust, respect, and mutual support. Strong, loving relationships enhance the quality of life and contribute to overall well-being.

- Building Community: The love shared within families and communities fosters a sense of unity and collective responsibility. Loving relationships contribute to the creation of supportive and compassionate communities.

Love and Spiritual Fulfillment

For many people, love is closely tied to spiritual fulfillment. It provides a sense of connection to something greater than oneself and fosters a sense of peace and contentment.

1. Spiritual Connection

Love often involves a spiritual connection that transcends the physical and emotional realms.

- Transcendent Love: The experience of deep, unconditional love can feel transcendent, providing a sense of connection to a higher power or universal truth. This spiritual dimension of love enhances its significance and impact on our lives.

- Inner Peace: Loving relationships contribute to inner peace and spiritual fulfillment. The sense of harmony and balance derived from loving connections fosters a deeper sense of spiritual well-being.

2. Spiritual Practices

Engaging in spiritual practices with loved ones can deepen the sense of purpose and fulfillment derived from love.

- Shared Practices: Shared spiritual practices, such as prayer, meditation, or attending religious services, strengthen the bond between individuals and enhance their sense of spiritual connection and purpose.

- Acts of Service: Acts of love and service to others are often seen as expressions of spiritual devotion. Engaging in charitable activities and supporting those in need fosters a sense of spiritual fulfillment and purpose.

Love is a fundamental source of meaning and purpose in life. It shapes our identity, guides our actions, and enriches our experiences. By fostering personal growth, enhancing emotional well-being, and contributing to societal harmony, love plays a crucial role in creating a fulfilling and meaningful life.

As we continue our exploration in this book, we will delve into the ways romantic love contributes to personal growth and fulfillment, examining how love can be a catalyst for self-discovery and life satisfaction. Through this journey, we aim to uncover the many layers that contribute to our understanding of love, enriching our appreciation of this powerful and transformative force in human life.

Love and Purpose

Love is often heralded as the most profound human experience, capable of providing deep fulfillment and a sense of purpose. Understanding and experiencing love in its many forms can significantly enhance the quality of our lives, offering emotional richness, personal growth, and a connection to something greater than ourselves. In this chapter, we will discuss how love contributes to a more fulfilling existence, exploring its impact on our daily lives, relationships, and overall sense of purpose.

The Multifaceted Nature of Love

Love manifests in various forms, each contributing uniquely to our sense of fulfillment and purpose. These forms include romantic love, familial love, platonic love, and self-love.

1. Romantic Love

Romantic love involves deep emotional and physical connections, often characterized by passion, intimacy, and commitment.

- Emotional Intimacy: Romantic love provides a sense of emotional intimacy and connection, which fulfills our need for closeness and understanding. Sharing life's joys and challenges with a partner enriches our experiences and provides emotional support.

- Growth and Commitment: Romantic relationships often encourage personal growth and mutual support. The commitment involved in maintaining a healthy romantic relationship fosters responsibility, trust, and long-term fulfillment.

2. Familial Love

Familial love, the bond between family members, is foundational to our emotional development and well-being.

- Unconditional Support: Familial love offers a source of unconditional support and acceptance. The bonds between parents and children, siblings, and extended family members provide a secure foundation that nurtures emotional health and stability.

- Legacy and Continuity: Familial relationships connect us to our past and future, offering a sense of legacy and continuity. The traditions and values passed down through generations contribute to a meaningful and enriched life.

3. Platonic Love

Platonic love, the affection between friends, plays a crucial role in our social lives and personal fulfillment.

- Companionship and Joy: Friendships provide companionship and joy, enriching our daily lives. The shared experiences and mutual support found in friendships enhance our happiness and sense of belonging.

- Emotional Resilience: Friends offer a valuable support network, helping us navigate life's challenges and celebrating our successes. This emotional resilience contributes to overall well-being and life satisfaction.

4. Self-Love

Self-love involves recognizing and valuing one's own worth, fostering a healthy relationship with oneself.

- Self-Acceptance: Practicing self-love encourages self-acceptance and self-compassion. Accepting ourselves with all our strengths and weaknesses fosters a positive self-image and emotional well-being.

- Personal Growth: Self-love motivates us to pursue personal growth and self-improvement. Investing in our well-being and development leads to a more fulfilling and purpose-driven life.

How Love Enhances Daily Life

Experiencing love in its various forms enriches our daily lives, providing emotional support, joy, and a sense of belonging.

1. Emotional Support and Stability

Love provides a reliable source of emotional support and stability, helping us navigate life's ups and downs.

- Stress Reduction: The emotional support offered by loved ones reduces stress and promotes mental health. Knowing that there are people who care about us provides a sense of security and comfort.

- Emotional Balance: Loving relationships contribute to emotional balance, helping us maintain a positive outlook even in challenging times. The empathy and understanding of loved ones foster emotional resilience and well-being.

2. Joy and Happiness

Love brings joy and happiness into our lives, enhancing our overall sense of well-being.

- Shared Experiences: Sharing joyful experiences with loved ones amplifies our happiness. Celebrating achievements, enjoying leisure activities, and creating memories together enrich our lives and foster deeper connections.

- Daily Affection: Simple acts of affection, such as hugs, kind words, and spending quality time together, contribute to daily happiness. These expressions of love create a nurturing and positive environment.

3. Sense of Belonging

Love fosters a sense of belonging, connecting us to others and creating a supportive community.

- Social Connection: Loving relationships provide a sense of social connection, which is essential for emotional health. Being part of a loving community enhances our sense of belonging and reduces feelings of loneliness.

- Collective Identity: Love connects us to a collective identity, whether it's within a family, a circle of friends, or a community. This connection provides a sense of purpose and reinforces our values and beliefs.

Love as a Catalyst for Personal Growth

Understanding and experiencing love can be a powerful catalyst for personal growth, encouraging self-discovery, self-improvement, and the pursuit of meaningful goals.

1. Self-Discovery and Understanding

Love encourages self-discovery and understanding, helping us explore our identity and values.

- Reflective Relationships: Loving relationships act as mirrors, reflecting our strengths, weaknesses, and true selves. The feedback and insights from loved ones promote self-awareness and personal growth.

- Exploring Values: Love prompts us to reflect on our values and priorities. The experiences and interactions within loving relationships help us understand what truly matters to us, guiding our personal and moral development.

2. Encouragement and Motivation

Love provides the encouragement and motivation needed to pursue personal and professional goals.

- Supportive Environment: The support and belief of loved ones create an environment that fosters ambition and perseverance. Knowing that others believe in our potential motivates us to strive for success.

- Overcoming Challenges: Love enhances our resilience, helping us overcome challenges and setbacks. The encouragement and support from loved ones provide the strength needed to persist and achieve our goals.

3. Embracing Change

Love encourages us to embrace change and take positive steps toward self-improvement.

- Growth Mindset: Loving relationships foster a growth mindset, where individuals are open to learning and self-improvement. The desire to be a better partner, friend, or family member motivates personal development.

- Constructive Feedback: The constructive feedback from loved ones helps us recognize areas for improvement. This feedback, given with love and concern, promotes positive change and self-growth.

Love and Purpose in Life

Love gives life a profound sense of purpose, guiding our actions and decisions, and enriching our existence.

1. Purpose-Driven Actions

Love guides our actions and decisions, aligning them with our values and goals.

- Meaningful Contributions: Love inspires us to make meaningful contributions to the lives of others. Whether it's through acts of kindness, support, or service, love motivates us to have a positive impact on the world.

- Aligned Goals: The goals we pursue are often aligned with the well-being of our loved ones. Love encourages us to set and achieve goals that not only fulfill our desires but also benefit those we care about.

2. Legacy and Impact

Love motivates us to leave a lasting legacy and make a meaningful impact on future generations.

- Building a Legacy: The love we have for our family and community inspires us to create a positive legacy. This may involve raising compassionate and responsible children, contributing to our community, or supporting causes we care about.

- Long-Term Impact: Love drives us to think about the long-term impact of our actions. The desire to create a better world for future generations gives our lives a sense of purpose and direction.

Understanding and experiencing love in its many forms significantly contribute to a more fulfilling existence. Love enriches our daily lives, fosters personal growth, and provides a profound sense of purpose. By embracing love and nurturing our relationships, we can create a life filled with meaning, joy, and fulfillment.

As we continue our exploration in this book, we will delve into the ways romantic love contributes to personal growth and fulfillment, examining how love can be a catalyst for self-discovery and life satisfaction. Through this journey, we aim to uncover the many layers that contribute to our understanding of love, enriching our appreciation of this powerful and transformative force in human life.

CHAPTER 10

THE FUTURE OF LOVE

As society continues to evolve, so too do our concepts and experiences of romantic love and relationships. Technological advancements, cultural shifts, and changing social norms are all influencing how we form, maintain, and perceive romantic connections. In this chapter, we will speculate on the future trends in romantic relationships and the evolution of love, exploring how these changes may shape our understanding and experience of love in the years to come.

The Impact of Technology on Romantic Relationships

Technology is rapidly transforming the way we connect and interact with others, and this includes romantic relationships. From online dating to virtual reality, technological innovations are reshaping the landscape of love.

1. Online Dating and Digital Matchmaking

Online dating has become a mainstream method for meeting potential partners, and its influence is likely to grow.

- Algorithmic Matchmaking: Advances in artificial intelligence and data analytics are improving the accuracy and effectiveness of matchmaking algorithms. These algorithms can analyze vast amounts of data to predict compatibility and suggest potential matches, making the process of finding a partner more efficient and personalized.

- Niche Dating Platforms: The rise of niche dating platforms tailored to specific interests, lifestyles, and demographics allows individuals to find partners who share their values and preferences. This trend is likely to continue, providing more options for people seeking like-minded partners.

2. Virtual and Augmented Reality

Virtual and augmented reality technologies are creating new possibilities for romantic interactions and experiences.

- Virtual Dates: Virtual reality (VR) can facilitate immersive, interactive dates for couples who are geographically separated. VR environments can mimic real-world settings, allowing couples to experience activities together, such as dining at a virtual restaurant or exploring a virtual city.

- Augmented Reality (AR) Experiences: AR can enhance real-world experiences by overlaying digital information and interactions. For example, couples could use AR to leave virtual notes for each other in their shared living space or to create interactive, personalized experiences.

3. Communication and Connectivity

Advancements in communication technology are making it easier for couples to stay connected, regardless of distance.

- Instant Messaging and Video Calls: The ubiquity of instant messaging and video calls enables couples to maintain close communication, even when they are apart. These technologies help bridge the gap created by physical distance and foster emotional intimacy.

- Wearable Devices: Wearable devices that track health metrics and send haptic feedback can enhance the sense of connection between partners. For example, a wearable device could send a gentle vibration to a partner's wrist as a signal of affection or as a reminder to think about each other.

Changing Social Norms and Cultural Shifts

Social norms and cultural attitudes toward romantic relationships are continuously evolving, influencing how love is experienced and expressed.

1. Diverse Relationship Structures

The traditional model of monogamous, heterosexual relationships is expanding to include a variety of relationship structures.

- Polyamory and Open Relationships: There is growing acceptance of polyamorous and open relationships, where individuals maintain multiple romantic connections with the knowledge and consent of all parties involved. These relationship structures emphasize transparency, communication, and consent.

- Non-Traditional Family Units: Non-traditional family units, such as co-parenting arrangements and communal living, are becoming more common. These arrangements reflect a shift towards more flexible and inclusive definitions of family and partnership.

2. Gender Roles and Equality

Evolving gender roles and increasing emphasis on gender equality are reshaping romantic relationships.

- Shared Responsibilities: As gender roles become more fluid, there is a greater emphasis on shared responsibilities within relationships. This includes equitable distribution of household chores, financial contributions, and parenting duties.

- Empowerment and Autonomy: Greater emphasis on gender equality empowers individuals to pursue their goals and aspirations, both within and outside of their relationships. This shift fosters more balanced and mutually supportive partnerships.

3. Cultural Diversity and Globalization

Globalization and cultural exchange are influencing romantic relationships, leading to greater diversity and cross-cultural connections.

- Intercultural Relationships: Increased mobility and digital connectivity facilitate intercultural relationships, where partners come from different cultural backgrounds. These relationships promote cultural exchange and understanding, enriching the experience of love.

- Blended Traditions: Couples in intercultural relationships often blend traditions and practices from their respective cultures, creating unique and personalized expressions of love and partnership.

The Role of Personal Development and Self-Love

As society places greater emphasis on personal development and self-care, the concepts of self-love and personal growth are becoming integral to romantic relationships.

1. Self-Love and Relationship Health

Understanding and practicing self-love is essential for maintaining healthy and fulfilling relationships.

- Emotional Independence: Cultivating self-love fosters emotional independence, allowing individuals to enter relationships from a place of wholeness and self-assurance. This independence enhances relationship health by reducing dependency and fostering mutual respect.

- Healthy Boundaries: Practicing self-love involves setting and maintaining healthy boundaries. Clear boundaries protect individual well-being and promote balanced, respectful interactions within relationships.

2. Personal Growth and Mutual Support

Personal growth and mutual support are key components of thriving romantic relationships.

- Growth-Oriented Relationships: Relationships that prioritize personal growth encourage partners to support each other's development and aspirations. This growth-oriented approach fosters resilience, adaptability, and long-term satisfaction.

- Mutual Empowerment: In growth-oriented relationships, partners empower each other to pursue their goals and dreams. This mutual empowerment creates a dynamic and supportive partnership that evolves and strengthens over time.

Environmental and Societal Factors

Environmental and societal factors, such as urbanization, climate change, and economic conditions, also influence the future of romantic relationships.

1. Urbanization and Mobility

Urbanization and increased mobility are changing the dynamics of romantic relationships.

- Transient Lifestyles: Urban environments and the demands of modern life often lead to transient lifestyles, where individuals frequently move for work or education. This mobility can challenge traditional relationship structures but also offers opportunities for new connections and experiences.

- Co-Living Spaces: The rise of co-living spaces, where individuals share communal living arrangements, fosters social interaction and can facilitate the formation of romantic relationships. These spaces provide a sense of community and support, enhancing emotional well-being.

2. Climate Change and Sustainability

Climate change and environmental sustainability are emerging as important considerations in romantic relationships.

- Eco-Conscious Partnerships: Couples are increasingly prioritizing sustainability and environmental consciousness in their relationships. Shared values around sustainability can strengthen bonds and promote joint efforts to reduce environmental impact.

- Resilience and Adaptability: As climate change affects living conditions and resources, relationships that prioritize resilience and adaptability will be better equipped to navigate environmental challenges. Collaborative problem-solving and mutual support are crucial in these contexts.

3. Economic Conditions

Economic conditions and job markets influence romantic relationships and partnership dynamics.

- Financial Stability: Economic stability is a significant factor in relationship satisfaction. Couples facing economic uncertainty may experience stress and strain, highlighting the importance of financial planning and mutual support.

- Work-Life Balance: Balancing career demands with relationship needs is increasingly important. Flexible work arrangements and a focus on work-life balance can enhance relationship quality and personal fulfillment.

The future of love is shaped by a complex interplay of technological advancements, changing social norms, cultural shifts, and environmental factors. As we navigate these changes, the core principles of love—empathy, compassion, mutual support, and personal growth—remain constant. By embracing these principles and adapting to new realities, we can continue to cultivate deep, meaningful, and fulfilling romantic relationships.

As we conclude our exploration in this book, we recognize that love is a dynamic and evolving force that enriches our lives in countless ways. Through understanding and experiencing love in its many forms, we gain insight into the essence of our humanity and the transformative power of love in shaping our world.

The Future of Love

The modern world presents both challenges and opportunities for enhancing romantic love and relationships. As we navigate technological advancements, changing social norms, and shifting cultural landscapes, understanding and fostering love in contemporary contexts becomes increasingly important. This chapter will discuss potential challenges and opportunities for enhancing love in the modern world, offering insights into how we can adapt and thrive in our romantic relationships amidst these evolving dynamics.

Challenges to Enhancing Love in the Modern World

1. Technological Distractions

The pervasive presence of technology in our lives can create distractions and hinder deep, meaningful connections in romantic relationships.

- Digital Overload: Constant connectivity and the influx of information from smartphones, social media, and other digital platforms can divert attention away from partners. This digital overload can reduce the quality of interactions and intimacy.

- Reduced Face-to-Face Interaction: Reliance on digital communication can lead to a decrease in face-to-face interactions, which are crucial for building emotional intimacy and understanding. The lack of physical presence can weaken emotional bonds.

2. Work-Life Balance

The demands of modern work life can strain romantic relationships, making it challenging to maintain a healthy balance between career and personal life.

- Long Working Hours: Long working hours and high job demands can limit the time and energy available for nurturing romantic relationships. This imbalance can lead to neglect and emotional distance between partners.

- Stress and Burnout: Work-related stress and burnout can negatively impact relationship quality. The emotional and physical toll of work stress can reduce patience, empathy, and the ability to engage meaningfully with a partner.

3. Changing Social Norms

Evolving social norms around gender roles, relationship structures, and individual autonomy can create both opportunities and conflicts in romantic relationships.

- Redefining Gender Roles: As traditional gender roles evolve, couples may struggle to navigate new dynamics and expectations. Balancing equality and traditional expectations can create tension and require ongoing negotiation.

- Acceptance of Diverse Relationships: While there is growing acceptance of diverse relationship structures (such as polyamory and same-sex relationships), societal biases and prejudices can still create challenges for those who do not conform to traditional norms.

4. Economic Pressures

Economic pressures and financial instability can strain romantic relationships and impact overall relationship satisfaction.

- Financial Stress: Economic instability and financial stress can create conflict and tension in relationships.

Disagreements over money management and financial goals can erode trust and intimacy.

- Access to Resources: Economic disparities can limit access to resources that support relationship health, such as counseling services, leisure activities, and quality time together.

Opportunities for Enhancing Love in the Modern World

1. Leveraging Technology for Connection

While technology can be a distraction, it also offers opportunities to enhance connection and intimacy in romantic relationships.

- Digital Communication Tools: Video calls, instant messaging, and social media can help couples stay connected, especially in long-distance relationships. These tools provide convenient ways to share experiences and maintain emotional closeness.

- Relationship Apps and Resources: There are numerous apps and online resources designed to support relationship health. These include tools for improving communication, tracking relationship milestones, and accessing counseling services.

2. Promoting Work-Life Balance

Achieving a healthy work-life balance is essential for maintaining strong romantic relationships.

- Flexible Work Arrangements: Employers are increasingly recognizing the importance of work-life balance and offering flexible work arrangements, such as remote work and flexible hours. These arrangements can provide more time for partners to spend together.

- Prioritizing Quality Time: Couples can prioritize quality time by setting boundaries around work and dedicating time for shared activities and meaningful interactions. This intentional focus on relationship time can strengthen emotional bonds.

3. Embracing Changing Social Norms

Adapting to changing social norms can enhance relationship satisfaction and personal fulfillment.

- Equality and Partnership: Embracing gender equality and partnership in relationships can lead to more balanced and supportive dynamics. Sharing responsibilities and decision-making fosters mutual respect and collaboration.

- Acceptance and Inclusivity: Promoting acceptance and inclusivity for diverse relationship structures can create a more supportive environment for all couples. Recognizing and respecting different relationship choices enhances societal well-being and individual happiness.

4. Addressing Economic Pressures

Proactively addressing economic pressures can reduce stress and improve relationship quality.

- Financial Planning: Couples can benefit from joint financial planning and goal-setting. Creating a shared budget, saving for future goals, and managing debt together can reduce financial stress and promote unity.

- Access to Support Services: Seeking financial counseling and relationship support services can help couples navigate economic challenges. These resources provide guidance and strategies for managing finances and maintaining relationship health.

Fostering Love and Intimacy in Contemporary Relationships

1. Effective Communication

Effective communication is the foundation of a healthy and fulfilling relationship.

- Active Listening: Practicing active listening involves fully focusing on and understanding a partner's perspective without interrupting or judging. This approach fosters empathy and strengthens emotional connection.

- Open and Honest Dialogue: Encouraging open and honest dialogue about feelings, needs, and concerns promotes trust and intimacy. Regular check-ins and open conversations help partners stay connected and address issues before they escalate.

2. Prioritizing Emotional and Physical Intimacy

Emotional and physical intimacy are crucial for maintaining a strong romantic bond.

- Emotional Intimacy: Building emotional intimacy involves sharing thoughts, feelings, and experiences with a partner. Engaging in meaningful conversations, expressing appreciation, and showing vulnerability foster deeper emotional connections.

- Physical Intimacy: Physical intimacy, including affectionate touch, sexual activity, and shared physical activities, enhances relationship satisfaction. Prioritizing physical closeness helps maintain a strong emotional bond.

3. Cultivating Shared Interests and Activities

Engaging in shared interests and activities strengthens the connection between partners.

- Hobbies and Activities: Participating in hobbies and activities that both partners enjoy creates opportunities for bonding and shared experiences. Whether it's traveling, cooking, or playing sports, shared interests enhance relationship satisfaction.

- Quality Time: Dedicating regular quality time for shared activities, date nights, and special moments fosters intimacy and connection. Making time for each other amidst busy schedules reinforces the importance of the relationship.

4. Seeking Professional Support

Professional support can provide valuable insights and strategies for enhancing relationship health.

- Couples Counseling: Couples counseling offers a safe space to address relationship challenges, improve communication, and strengthen emotional bonds. Professional guidance can help partners navigate conflicts and enhance their connection.

- Relationship Workshops: Attending relationship workshops and seminars provides opportunities to learn new skills and strategies for maintaining a healthy relationship. These programs offer tools for improving communication, intimacy, and overall relationship satisfaction.

The modern world presents both challenges and opportunities for enhancing love and romantic relationships. By leveraging technology, promoting work-life balance, embracing changing social norms, and addressing economic pressures, couples can navigate contemporary dynamics and foster deeper, more fulfilling connections. Effective communication, prioritizing intimacy, cultivating shared interests, and seeking professional support are essential strategies for maintaining strong and healthy relationships.

As we conclude our exploration in this book, we recognize that love is a dynamic and evolving force that enriches our lives in countless ways. Through understanding and experiencing love in its many forms, we gain insight into the essence of our humanity and the transformative power of love in shaping our world. By embracing the opportunities and addressing the challenges of the modern world, we can continue to cultivate deep, meaningful, and fulfilling romantic relationships that stand the test of time.

THE NATURE, CHEMISTRY, AND SOURCES OF ROMANTIC LOVE

Summary of Key Findings and Insights

Throughout this book, we have explored the multifaceted nature of romantic love, delving into its biological, psychological, cultural, and spiritual dimensions. We have examined how love influences personal growth, relationship dynamics, and societal well-being. Here, we summarize the key findings and insights about the nature, chemistry, and sources of romantic love.

1. The Nature of Romantic Love

Romantic love is a complex and dynamic emotion that encompasses various forms, including passionate, companionate, and unconditional love. It is characterized by deep emotional connections, physical attraction, and a sense of commitment and partnership.

- Passionate Love: This form of love is marked by intense emotions, physical attraction, and a strong desire for closeness and intimacy. It often dominates the early stages of a romantic relationship.

- Companionate Love: Over time, passionate love may evolve into companionate love, which is characterized by deep emotional bonds, mutual respect, and a sense of partnership. This form of love emphasizes stability, trust, and long-term commitment.

2. The Chemistry of Love

The experience of romantic love is deeply rooted in our biology, driven by complex neurochemical processes that influence our emotions, behaviors, and connections with others.

- Neurotransmitters and Hormones: Key chemicals such as dopamine, oxytocin, serotonin, and endorphins play crucial roles in the formation and maintenance of romantic love. These chemicals are responsible for the feelings of pleasure, attachment, and emotional stability associated with love.

- Stages of Love: The chemistry of love varies across different stages of a relationship, from the initial attraction and infatuation to long-term attachment and bonding. Each stage is influenced by specific neurochemical changes that shape our experiences and behaviors.

3. Sources of Romantic Love

The sources of romantic love are diverse, encompassing biological, psychological, cultural, and spiritual factors.

- Biological Foundations: Evolutionary theories suggest that romantic love has adaptive functions, promoting mate selection, reproduction, and the survival of offspring. Biological processes and hormonal changes play a central role in the experience of love.

- Psychological Dimensions: Psychological theories emphasize the components of attachment, intimacy, and commitment in romantic relationships. Love is seen as a key factor in emotional well-being, personal growth, and relationship satisfaction.

- Cultural Influences: Cultural norms and societal expectations shape how romantic love is perceived and expressed. Media, literature, and social media play significant roles in influencing modern concepts of love and relationships.

- Spiritual Dimensions: Many religious and spiritual traditions view love as a divine force that transcends the physical and emotional realms. Understanding love from a spiritual perspective can enrich our appreciation of its transformative power.

Implications for Personal Growth, Relationships, and Society

Understanding the nature, chemistry, and sources of romantic love has profound implications for personal growth, relationship dynamics, and societal well-being.

1. Personal Growth

Love is a powerful catalyst for personal growth and self-discovery. It encourages introspection, fosters self-acceptance, and motivates individuals to strive for self-improvement.

- Self-Discovery: Loving relationships act as mirrors, reflecting our true selves and prompting us to explore our identity, values, and aspirations. This process of self-discovery enhances our understanding and appreciation of ourselves.

- Emotional Resilience: The support and encouragement provided by loving relationships enhance emotional resilience, helping individuals navigate life's challenges and pursue their goals with confidence and determination.

2. Relationship Dynamics

Understanding the dynamics of love can help individuals cultivate healthier, more fulfilling relationships.

Effective communication, mutual support, and emotional intimacy are key components of successful romantic relationships.

- Communication and Intimacy: Effective communication and emotional intimacy are essential for building strong, lasting relationships. Practicing active listening, empathy, and open dialogue fosters deeper connections and mutual understanding.

- Mutual Support and Growth: Healthy relationships are characterized by mutual support and shared growth. Partners who encourage and support each other's personal and professional aspirations create a dynamic and resilient partnership.

3. Societal Well-Being

Love plays a crucial role in promoting societal well-being by fostering social cohesion, compassion, and a sense of community. Cultivating love and compassion in personal relationships can have far-reaching effects on society as a whole.

- Social Cohesion and Community: Loving relationships strengthen social bonds and contribute to the formation of supportive, interconnected communities. This social cohesion enhances collective well-being and promotes social harmony.

- Compassion and Empathy: Love fosters compassion and empathy, encouraging individuals to consider the well-being of others and act in ways that promote social justice and collective good. This moral dimension of love is essential for creating a just and equitable society.

The exploration of romantic love reveals its profound impact on individual lives, relationships, and society. Understanding the nature, chemistry, and sources of love enriches our appreciation of this powerful and transformative force. Love, in its many forms, provides deep emotional fulfillment, fosters personal growth, and promotes societal well-being.

As we navigate the complexities of the modern world, embracing love and nurturing our relationships becomes increasingly important. By cultivating empathy, compassion, and mutual support, we can create deeper, more meaningful connections and contribute to a more harmonious and prosperous society.

Ultimately, love is a dynamic and evolving force that enriches our lives in countless ways. Through understanding and experiencing love, we gain insight into the essence of our humanity and the potential for transformation and fulfillment. By embracing the opportunities and addressing the challenges of the modern world, we can continue to cultivate deep, meaningful, and lasting romantic relationships that stand the test of time.

Key Findings and Insights About Romantic Love

Throughout this exploration of romantic love, we have uncovered its complex and multifaceted nature, examined the biological and chemical processes that underpin it, and considered the various sources and influences that shape our experience of love.

1. The Nature of Romantic Love

Romantic love is a dynamic and multi-dimensional experience characterized by deep emotional connections, physical attraction, and a sense of commitment. It can manifest in different forms, including passionate, companionate, and unconditional love, each contributing uniquely to our relationships and emotional well-being.

2. The Chemistry of Love

The experience of romantic love is deeply rooted in our biology, driven by a complex interplay of neurotransmitters and hormones such as dopamine, oxytocin, serotonin, and endorphins. These chemicals influence our feelings of pleasure, attachment, and emotional stability, varying across different stages of a relationship from initial attraction to long-term bonding.

3. Sources of Romantic Love

Romantic love arises from a combination of biological, psychological, cultural, and spiritual factors:

- Biological Foundations: Evolutionary theories suggest that romantic love has adaptive functions, promoting mate selection, reproduction, and the survival of offspring.

- Psychological Dimensions: Psychological theories emphasize attachment, intimacy, and commitment as key components of romantic love, which are crucial for emotional well-being and relationship satisfaction.

- Cultural Influences: Cultural norms, media, literature, and social media shape how romantic love is perceived and expressed, influencing modern concepts of relationships.

- Spiritual Dimensions: Many religious and spiritual traditions view love as a divine force that transcends the physical and emotional realms, offering a deeper understanding of its transformative power.

Implications for Personal Growth, Relationships, and Society

Understanding the nature, chemistry, and sources of romantic love has significant implications for personal growth, relationship dynamics, and societal well-being.

1. Personal Growth

Love serves as a powerful catalyst for personal growth and self-discovery:

- Self-Discovery: Loving relationships prompt introspection, helping individuals explore their identity, values, and aspirations, thereby enhancing self-understanding and appreciation.

- Emotional Resilience: The support and encouragement from loving relationships bolster emotional resilience, aiding individuals in navigating life's challenges and pursuing their goals with confidence.

2. Relationship Dynamics

Insight into the dynamics of love can help cultivate healthier, more fulfilling relationships:

- Communication and Intimacy: Effective communication and emotional intimacy are crucial for building strong relationships. Practices such as active listening, empathy, and open dialogue foster deeper connections and mutual understanding.

- Mutual Support and Growth: Healthy relationships are marked by mutual support and shared growth. Partners who encourage each other's aspirations create dynamic and resilient partnerships.

3. Societal Well-Being

Love contributes to societal well-being by fostering social cohesion, compassion, and a sense of community:

- Social Cohesion and Community: Loving relationships strengthen social bonds, contributing to the formation of supportive, interconnected communities and enhancing collective well-being.

- Compassion and Empathy: Love fosters compassion and empathy, prompting individuals to consider the well-being of others and act in ways that promote social justice and collective good, which are essential for a just and equitable society.

The exploration of romantic love reveals its profound impact on individual lives, relationships, and society. Understanding the nature, chemistry, and sources of love enriches our appreciation of this powerful and transformative force. Love provides deep emotional fulfillment, fosters personal growth, and promotes societal well-being.

In the modern world, embracing love and nurturing our relationships is increasingly important. By cultivating empathy, compassion, and mutual support, we can create deeper, more meaningful connections and contribute to a more harmonious and prosperous society. Ultimately, love is a dynamic and evolving force that enriches our lives in countless ways. Through understanding and experiencing love, we gain insight into the essence of our humanity and the potential for transformation and fulfillment. By addressing the challenges and seizing the opportunities of the modern world, we can continue to cultivate deep, meaningful, and lasting romantic relationships that stand the test of time.